KU-607-252

THE STORY
OF
SCOTLAND'S
HILLS

BY THE SAME AUTHOR

The Island Hills

Scotland
(Panorama-Books Series)

The Central Highlands
(Scottish Mountaineering Club District Guide Book)

Glens and Straths of Scotland

Enjoying Scotland

THE STORY
OF
SCOTLAND'S
HILLS

CAMPBELL STEVEN

ROBERT HALE · LONDON

© Campbell Steven 1975
First published in Great Britain 1975

ISBN 0 7091 4975 1

Robert Hale & Company
Clerkenwell House
Clerkenwell Green
London EC1R 0HT

Filmset by Specialised Offset Services Limited, Liverpool
and printed and bound in Great Britain by
Redwood Burn Limited
Trowbridge & Esher

CONTENTS

ILLUSTRATIONS

*Photographs taken by the author except those
specially mentioned*

ACKNOWLEDGEMENTS

It would be impossible to write any adequate story of Scotland's hills without frequent reference to *The Scottish Mountaineering Club Journal*. The wealth of material to be found in the pages of its thirty volumes is virtually inexhaustible and offers endless armchair enjoyment to the enthusiast. I am especially indebted to the Editor, Mr Robin N. Campbell, for permission to draw on it and also to make use of several photographs. In particular grateful mention must be made of Professor D.B. Horn's fascinating article 'The Origins of Mountaineering in Scotland' (Vol. 38, No. 157), which indicates a number of early sources of information, while for three actual quotations I should like to thank a former Editor, Dr G.F. Dutton, and also Mr Adam Watson senior and Dr Adam Watson junior.

I should like to express also my sincere thanks to the following: Mr P.M. Gibbs, Region Controller, Ordnance Survey Scottish Region; Professor H.H. Lamb, of the University of East Anglia, for meteorological references; also to Messrs. D.R. Grant, superintendent, and N.F. Hirst, of the Meteorological Office, Edinburgh, for making available material on Clement Wragge and the Ben Nevis observatory, along with a print for use as illustration; the Secretary, Scottish Youth Hostels Association; the Keeper, National Library of Scotland; Mr D.M. Button, Honorary Secretary, the Ben Nevis Race Association; Messrs. J.B. Nimlin and Ken Attwood for information regarding Cairngorm stones; Mr J.C. Donaldson for up-to-date details of Munro's *Tables*, and Mr John Downie for recollections of the 52nd (Lowland) Division. Finally to Mr Seton Gordon for allowing me to quote from his book *The Charm of Skye* and to the following publishers for permission to use quotations as detailed in the text: William Blackwood & Sons Ltd, Cassell & Co. Ltd, Victor Gollancz Ltd, Hodder & Stoughton Ltd and Christy & Moore Ltd, Martin Secker & Warburg Ltd, H.F. & G. Witherby Ltd.

INTRODUCTION

No doubt it is presumptuous to call this the story of Scotland's hills, for who, after all, can say where that story should begin and where it should end? Certainly the gaps and deficiencies of this attempt will be only too obvious. For one thing there is no chapter on the geology of the hills, a subject probably best avoided by anyone who knows next to nothing about it. For another, the mention of Scottish mountaineers still actively on the scene has been kept to an absolute minimum for fairly obvious — and I hope sound — reasons. Similarly it is no more than a random selection of climbs that has been made, and that to fit the thread of the story; the places to look for lists and details are in the various specialised guide-books and the club journals.

The fact that at the time of writing a new, revised edition of Munro's *Tables* is being prepared for publication has caused a certain amount of difficulty; some of the heights of the hills are being amended and metric equivalents are being included. My apologies are offered for any inaccuracies which may have occurred because of these changes.

To
Iain G. Jack
companion of many memorable days
on the hills

1
The Setting

It is salutary — if a little disturbing — to pause for a moment and reflect how ready we are to take our Scottish hills for granted. Perhaps it is because they belong so intimately to the country's make-up, because they are so close-woven into the pattern of history. Whatever the reason, it is all too true that for the most part we fail lamentably to appreciate them as they deserve.

One of their chief attractions — their quite remarkable diversity of structure — is particularly easily overlooked. For instance there could hardly be more striking contrasts between, say, Ben Alder and An Teallach, or Cairn Gorm and Sgurr Alasdair, or the gentle grass dome of The Merrick and the sandstone pinnacles of Stack Polly, that "porcupine in a state of extreme irascibility"; fire and frost, rain and wind and ice have done their work well in vastly different ways since the first beginnings of time. Yet this extraordinary variety — unique surely for any country the size of Scotland — is not often mentioned and even less often emphasised.

Not that there is any need to be a geologist to take delight in all this; indeed it could be that that might even be a drawback — perhaps seeing too closely the results of glacier action, or speculating with over-much concern on the age of gneiss or basalt or pitchstone. Better possibly to enjoy the peaks as an out-and-out amateur on the scientific side, equipped simply with an appreciative eye for line and colour, and endeavouring to gain as close an acquaintance as possible with the high places at every season of the year. Thus the ordinary layman may have only the haziest idea of how the gabbro pinnacles of Sgurr nan Gillean came to be formed, or why they are so different from the tors of Ben Avon or the layered sandstone of the Old Man of Hoy; but at least he may still enjoy them to the full, either from a distance or as he delights in the feel of their texture in the course of a day's climbing.

The early visitors to the Highlands were not exactly complimentary about the appearance of the hills. General Wade's agent, Edward Burt, writing in 1725 or 1726, maintained that "The Summits of the highest Mountains are mostly destitute of Earth, and the huge naked Rocks, being just above the Heath, produce the disagreeable Appearance of a scabbed Head."* And Dr Johnson, less clinical if no less sour, produced his often-quoted definition of a Highland Ben as "a considerable protuberance."

Yet it would be hardly fair to class all tourists of those days as Philistines. Thomas Pennant, for instance, with that shrewdly observant eye of his, was surprisingly modern in some of his descriptions. Exactly as anyone today might do, he talked about the 'woolpack' formation of the rock-peaks of Arran, the piled monoliths of granite so familiar to those who enjoy the climbing problems of Cir Mhor and Goat Fell and Beinn Tarsuinn. He talked, too, with surprising accuracy of Liathach: "On the west side [of the glen] is an amazing mountain steeply sloping, composed of a whitish marble, so extensive, smooth, glossy and even, as to appear like an enormous sheet of ice; and is, I doubt not, as slippery. Our guide called the hill, Leacach." Observations easily appreciated by anyone who knows the steep terraces which fall like frozen waterfalls to Glen Torridon and make Liathach so formidable.

Another thirty years on, in 1803, a traveller dropping down Glen Shiel to Kintail is mightily impressed — as countless later visitors have been — by the steepness of the Five Sisters on the one hand and The Saddle on the other; probably by Sgurr Fhuaran in particular, as it has one of the longest continuous grass slopes in Britain: "I have never seen sublimer mountainous scenery than the tract between Cluony and Ratachan . . . and I was much gratified by surveying the majestic grandeur of the summits, on both sides of the road. It was an inclined wall, of such inaccessible height that no living creature would venture to scale it."

***Letters from a Gentleman in the North of Scotland* (London, 1754).

These ridges flanking Glen Shiel on both its north and its south sides are justly popular with hill-walkers these days for the way in which they conveniently link so many 'Munros'. But then there is such an abundance of long high-level expeditions up and down the country that this kind of choice is practically unlimited. For example, from Forest Lodge to Kingshouse — or, more recently, in the reverse direction on ski, making use of the White Corries chairlift — is one classic which affords tremendous views into the depths of Coire Ba and far out over Rannoch Moor; another long expedition is the 'ridging' of the nine 'Munros' and three additional 'tops' of the Fannichs, in Ross-shire; the seven highest Cairngorms have been traversed in a twenty-hour day, and if ambitions soar to still greater heights there is always the toughest marathon of all — the round of the Mamores, the Grey Corries, the Aonachs and Ben Nevis — 36 miles and 20,000 feet of climbing first accomplished in 23¼ hours by the late Philip Tranter in June 1964.

The ridges of Skye are, of course, unmatched for technical difficulty and sheer exhilaration. Yet the mainland has its well-varied choice to offer too, for instance on the sandstone of An Teallach and Liathach in Wester Ross, or the shattered, curving *arête* — particularly delectable under snow — which links Carn Mor Dearg with Ben Nevis and which affords such magnificent views of the latter's northern precipices. Finest of all — and demanding a great deal more respect than it is often given — is the north-flanking wall of Glencoe, the well-known Aonach Eagach, or 'notched ridge', which provides such a memorable expedition, especially working from the east towards the far views of the coast.

It is, however, in Skye that ridge-wandering reaches perfection. Often, even at the height of summer, it can be brutally cold; many a visitor from the South has had to return home with nothing but memories of driving mist and soaking, shivering rain. In the well-known words of Sheriff Nicolson,

> If you are a delicate man,
>   And of wetting your skin are shy,
> I'd have you know, before you go,
>   You had better not think of Skye.

And yet, when the sun does come out and the mists roll away, there is nothing anywhere quite like 'the Ridge'. Its features grow familiar — the spire of Sgurr Alasdair, the Inaccessible Pinnacle hunched like some great crouching dinosaur, the Bhasteir Tooth, the pinnacles of Sgurr nan Gillean; the rocks become rough and warm and friendly to the touch, and the views stretch out from the puzzling tangle of the mainland hills to the limitless sea-sparkle that sets off in avenues of light Rum and Canna and the Outer Isles.

The classic expedition of traversing the main Cuillin ridge in a day dates from 1911 and is now almost commonplace. And yet no amount of familiarity could really breed even a suggestion of contempt. As the late Frank Smythe graphically described it:

> From Garsbheinn the Coolins bend round in a noble parabola to Sgurr nan Gillean. Perhaps thirty peaks had to be traversed. It was a grand day's scrambling: now along some rocky edge; now over some tower; now down to some sunless gap with the loose stones whirring and jarring into the scree gullies on either hand. And always, on either hand, luminous horizons, moors, hills and sea.
>
> We climbed lethargically down the pinnacle ridge of Sgurr nan Gillean. Never shall I forget my craving for water; still less the moorland stream into which I plunged my hot face, and the feel and taste of the cold peaty water in my parched mouth. I forget how long we took: I think it was seventeen or eighteen hours. Someone has done it since in twelve, or less. The traverse of the Coolins is the grandest day's scrambling in Britain. Next time I shall lounge along like the lazy fellow I am.*

It is, perhaps, in the islands that is to be seen most clearly of all the extraordinary variety of our hills. In addition to the basalt and gabbro of the Black Cuillin, Skye has the Red Hills — tamely conical and rounded by comparison, their sides consisting mainly of steep granite screes. Away to the south, astride the entrance to the Firth of Clyde, Ailsa Craig on a sunny day shows off the sober, subtle colouring of its basaltic columns against the blue of the sea and the flashing white of its gannets. Arran has its 'woolpack' architecture, the great granite blocks inexorably severed and separated from each other by the action of the weather, sometimes along the

---

The Spirit of the Hills (Hodder & Stoughton, London, 1935).

A familiar hill overlooking Loch Marée: Slioch (3,217 feet)

A picturesque corrie of the Fannichs, Ross-shire: Loch Gorm
from the north ridge of An Coileachan

Black Mount country. The bridge over the River Ba
on the old Glencoe road

thinnest of fissures. By contrast, on the Paps of Jura the steep, sprawling screes are of quartzite — and when wet as slippery as ice to the climber in Vibram-soled boots.

Completely different again is the fluted pitchstone of the Sgurr of Eigg. Hugh Miller, the geologist, was duly captivated when he landed on the island from the *Betsey* over a century ago:

> The columns, as we pass on towards the west, diminish in size, and assume in many of the beds considerable variety of direction and form. In one bed they belly over with a curve, like the ribs of some wrecked vessel from which the planking has been torn away; in another they project in a straight line, like muskets planted slantways on the ground to receive a charge of cavalry; in others the inclination is inwards, like that of ranges of stakes placed in front of a sea-dyke, to break the violence of the waves; while in yet others they present, as in the eastern portion of the Scuir, the common vertical direction.*

Near by, the magnificent hills of Rum — a Cuillin ridge in miniature — have an assortment of geological structures, in sum total immensely satisfying for the climber. Away thence, to the north-west, to Strone Ulladale in Harris, with its immense overhanging face of close on 1,000 feet, "probably one of the half-score finest rock features in Britain"; north to the sandstone verticalities of the Old Man of Hoy; out west into the Atlantic to the sea-stacks of St Kilda, among the most dramatic in the world.

It is difficult indeed to imagine an assortment more varied, more remarkable, more attractive than that.

One development which, over the last half-century, has done much to introduce uniformity in place of variety, has been the work of the Forestry Commission. In 1919, when it was set up, the Commission was without a single tree or an acre of land to its name; today in Scotland plantations extend approximately to the million-acre mark. Whether or not all of this planting is really necessary is a complex question and one that is possibly best left to the experts. Yet one comment may perhaps be allowed and that is that the Commission seems reluctant to concede any merit at all in a treeless landscape, or that there can be any possible attraction in a completely

---

* The Cruise of the Betsey (1858).

barren hillside; it is almost as though it is taken for granted that serried ranks of conifers automatically improve a view, or at any rate cannot conceivably spoil it. Thus at Crianlarich the moorland approaches to Cruach Ardrain have suffered widespread invasion; that superb panorama from the A82 across Loch Tulla to the hills of the Black Mount and the Ben Starav group has been 'improved' by a growing screen actually between the road and the loch, and still farther on the wide sweep of the Moor of Rannoch had to have its plantation just where the outlook over it is best, north of Loch Ba.

For many, Rannoch Moor with its limitless acres of heather, its peat-hags and its slow-running burns, speaks expressively of all the solitary places of the Highlands, now unfortunately becoming so much fewer. Its atmosphere was admirably caught and portrayed by Neil Munro in *The New Road* as Ninian Campbell and Aeneas Macmaster looked out on it from Kingshouse Inn:

> The inn stood on a desert edge; behind rose up the scowling mountains of Glen Coe, so high and steep that even heather failed them, and their gullies sent down streams of stones instead of foam. Eastward, where the inn-front looked, the moor stretched flat and naked as a Sound; three days' march from end to end they said were on it — all untracked and desert-melancholy. Its nearer parts were green with boggy grass, on which the cannoch tuft — the cotton-sedge — was strewn like flakes of snow; distantly its hue was sombre — grey like ashes, blackened here and there with holes of peat. The end of it was lost in mist from which there jutted, like a skerry of the sea, Schiehallion.*

It is well that the Moor should be left as it is.

Inevitably several of the finest lochs have had to be sacrificed to some extent to the demands of hydro-electricity; on the whole, perhaps, these have not been ruined, although the 'tide-marks' which can be so glaringly obvious are disfigurements which no amount of tidying up can put to rights. Fortunately the threat which jeopardised Lochan Fada, set in the lonely 'wilderness area' to the north of Loch Maree, has so far not materialised; nor have hands yet been laid on Loch Coruisk or on Loch Avon, in the heart of the Cairngorms.

Undoubtedly one of the most distinctive features of all of the

---

* *The New Road* (William Blackwood, Edinburgh, 1930).

Scottish hills is the combination of remote corrie and captive lochan. Here again variety is almost unlimited. One thinks, for example, of Lochan Uaine, that one of the four Green Lochs in the Cairngorms which is cupped in almost formal symmetry on the Garbh Choire flank of Cairn Toul, and one sets it against the lochan in Coire Mhic Fhearchair, to the scree shores of which the triple 1,300-foot rock-buttresses, rugged quartzite and Torridonian sandstone, plunge so dramatically from the summit horseshoe of Beinn Eighe. The contrast could scarcely be more striking. Sometimes it is contended that the finest of all is Loch Toll an Lochain, overlooked as it is by the magnificent cirque of An Teallach's principal 'tops'. Sometimes the claims of the great eastern corrie of Lochnagar, with its lochan and crescent of cliffs, are confidently put forward. Yet again it is maintained that for sheer grandeur Coire Lagan and Coir' a' Ghrunnda in Skye are altogether unbeatable. The arguments could last indefinitely.

So, too, with the peaks themselves: Cir Mhor in Arran described as "aesthetically satisfying from every point in the compass owing to its Matterhorn-like detachment from its neighbours"; Slioch under fresh snow, glimpsed from among the scattered pines on Loch Maree-side; the lines of Askival and Allival in Rum, seen against a flaring sunset from the sands of Morar; light and shadow chasing each other across the battlements of Suilven's Grey Castle; the face of Buachaille Etive Mor, mist-girdled, catching the early sun beyond the edge of Rannoch Moor . . . Is it necessary to make a choice, or could it be satisfying enough just to acknowledge that after all discussion need have no end?

2
The Names of The Hills

Just as the configuration of the Scottish hills is right at the very heart of their character, so also is the rich variety of their names.

At first, admittedly, it is by no means obvious that there is anything particularly imaginative about the latter at all: when one tries deciphering the Gaelic sprawled with such gay abandon over the maps of the Highlands, the meanings seem mostly to be quite commonplace — usually just 'big' or 'little', 'black' perhaps, or 'red' or 'rough'. But delve deeper — even just a little deeper — and the rewards become more apparent. Before long one has begun to acquire a new and far livelier appreciation of the scenery and often enough of history as well.

This is an aspect of the Highland scene which, it seems to me, has been surprisingly neglected by the various tourist bodies. It is in fact a ready-made feature of interest, clamouring to be accorded due recognition. Yet it is one which, apart from a few rather feeble, half-hearted attempts — usually relegated ignominiously to appendices — has been given no worthy attention at all.

It is most unfortunate that so little light on the subject is to be derived from the efforts of the very early map-makers. They excelled at drawing innumerable shapely little molehills in approximately the right places, but paid scant heed to the addition of names. This is not really surprising, of course, for the difficulties they faced, with non-existent roads, hostile weather and above all a strange language, were almost insurmountable. Their failures emphasise the more the truly wonderful job done later on by those who made the Ordnance Survey maps, collecting and confirming literally countless local names and no doubt wrestling many a fall with pronunciations well-nigh impossible to reproduce.

Probably most visitors to Scotland and the Highlands are inclined at first to think of the mountain names as being prefixed automatically by Ben. This is not so. The Gaels used quite a selection of names, each having its own subtle shade of meaning, so that, generally speaking, it is not too difficult to tell from the map just what a hill is like. *Sgurr* or *sgorr* is usually a real peak, as shapely as any: for example Sgurr Alasdair in Skye, or that fine pair of summits above Ballachulish, Sgorr Dearg and Sgorr Dhonuill, or again the Sgurr of Eigg, dominating the brown moors at its base like some miniature island Matterhorn. At the other end of the scale, *meall* is a rounded, flat-topped hill — even, it is sometimes rendered, a 'lump' — of no great character at all. Among other descriptions, *stob* is a 'point', very often the subsidiary 'top' of a main peak; *sron* is a 'nose' or 'shoulder', while *aonach* is a 'ridge', as for instance in the celebrated Aonach Eagach, or 'notched ridge', above Glencoe.

Most commonly, of course, colours enter into the variegated, overall pattern. It is easy enough to appreciate how they must have fired the imagination of the people far back in the remote past. The following is a list of some of the commoner colours found in hill-names here, there and everywhere throughout the Highlands:

ban	— white or fair;	*gorm*	— blue, azure;
dubh	— black or dark;	*glas*	— grey, pale;
dearg	— red;	*geal*	— white, bright;
ruadh	— red, reddish;	*liath*	— grey;
buidhe	— yellow, golden;	*uaine*	— green;
	odhar	— dun-coloured, tawny.		

Curiously enough, for all the heather of late summer, I have never come across *corcurach*, 'purple', or even *donn*, 'brown'. Sometimes one is inclined to think that it was just any old colour that was chosen, but now and again the selection is obviously exactly right. For instance on Stob Ban, 'white top', in the Mamore hills, the upper screes of gleaming quartzite look almost like snow in certain lights. How often, too, when the clouds are low and trailing, the vague rolling slopes of the Monadh Liath live up to their name of 'grey moors'!

Very different but no less fascinating are the glimpses far back into the drifting mists of history afforded by the Norse elements of not a few of our mountain names. Inevitably, during the centuries when the Hebrides were occupied, lasting imprints were made. In particular in the islands and round the coast, where the peaks would be invaluable as landmarks to the roving viking seafarers, aptly descriptive names would come early into ordinary everyday use.

One such example is *sulur*, meaning 'pillar', a mountain name which crops up remarkably often on maps of Iceland — where the language has not moved on very far from its Old Norse origins. This is a component of Suilven (Sulur Bheinn), that splendidly isolated 'pillar mountain' of Sutherland which must have been so familiar to the navigator of many a marauding galley in viking times. Another similar Norse-Gaelic hybrid is Blaven (Blå Bheinn), 'blue mountain', familiar outlier of the main Cuillin Ridge in Skye. In another way yet no less interesting, it is surely no coincidence that Hecla, shapeliest hill in South Uist, should have its counterpart in Hekla, probably the best-known mountain in Iceland.

Almost worthy of a special study on its own account is *fjall*, ancient word for 'hill' or 'fell', which has remained the same into modern Icelandic and become *fjell* in Norwegian. This has produced the suffix '-val', to be seen in a great number of hill-names in the Hebrides, in the Long Island especially. Thus in Lewis we have Mealasbhal and Cracabhal; in Harris Ullaval, Stulaval, more than one Oreval, Roneval and many more; in North Uist Marrival and Eaval; in South Uist Stulaval again and Easaval; in Barra the highest point, Heaval. Even Goat Fell, well to the south in Arran, is said to be Geitafjall or 'goat hill'. Most familiar of all probably are the peaks of Rum, with the musical sounding names, Allival and Askival, Trallval, Ashval and Ruinsival. It is interesting all the same to note that only fifteen miles away across the Cuillin Sound the main Skye summits (apart from Blaven) have Gaelic rather than Norse names, although a possible blend is that of Sgurr nan Gillean, 'peak of ghylls or gullies'. Actually Norse influence in Skye, so far as other place-names are concerned, was so extensive that it is difficult to believe that the name Cuillin itself should be anything other than of Scandinavian origin. Martin Martin writing in 1695 refers to the 'Quillin hills', although some time seemingly fairly soon after that confusion was caused by the introduction of a possible association with the legendary Irish hero Cuchulainn. Thus Thomas Pennant in 1772 calls the Skye hills 'Cuchullin, Cullin, or Quillin'. There is uncertainty, admittedly, but to one inexpert way of thinking at any rate the Cuchulainn theory is too improbable to be accepted. A more reasonable explanation would appear to be quite simply derivation from the Old Norse word *Kjölen*, meaning 'high rocks'.

Dating, perhaps, from almost as far back in the blurred beginnings of history as do hill-names associated with colours, are those which have trees in their make-up. Among these, for example, is Beinn a' Chaoruinn at the west end of Loch Laggan, one 'hill in the rowan tree' among a number to be found here and there in the Highlands. One of the 'tops' in the Mamores is Sgor an Oubhair, 'peak of the yew tree', while the scenic attractions of Glen Iubhair are well known to those familiar with the approaches to the fine rock walls of Garth Bheinn of Ardgour. Climbers who frequent the rock and snow playgrounds of Glencoe are often attracted to the problems of Stob Coire nam Beith, meaning picturesquely the 'top of the birch tree corrie.' In the Cairngorms it would be surprising indeed if the Scots pines which go to the making of the great forests of Rothiemurchus and Mar were given no mention: thus there is Glen Giusachan, reaching far back into the fastness of Cairn Toul, and in it the River Giusachan, although there seems to be no actual 'hill of the pines' thereabout at any rate. Near the head of Loch Shiel, and a picturesque component of the view from Glenfinnan, there is a fine Sgurr Ghiubhsachain.

Birds and animals also have made their contributions, although names of the former are less commonly encountered than might perhaps have been expected. In the Lawers group Meall nan Tarmachan, 'hill of the ptarmigan', is the highest of the craggy range of summits so well seen from Killin, while one of the subsidiary 'tops' on the other side of Ben Lawers itself is Creag an Fhithich, 'raven's crag'. At the head of Loch Etive — pleasantly out of the ordinary — there is the 'mountain of sandpipers', Beinn Trilleachan. On Sgurr Nid na h-Iolaire, 'peak of the eagle's nest' — the name given locally to a prominent nose of The Saddle, in Glen Shiel — golden eagles are reputed to have an eyrie. Well to

the south in Galloway, Benyellary, the long moorland
shoulder of The Merrick, is said to be a corruption of Beinn na
h-Iolaire, 'peak of the eagle'; this is not in the least unlikely,
for certainly in the earlier part of last century eagles were very
numerous in these remote Kirkcudbrightshire hills and it is
said that there are still three or four pairs breeding there.
Rather more surprising is the name Loch nan Stuirteag, 'loch
of the black-headed gulls', at the edge of the lonely Great
Moss in the Cairngorms; this seems to have been given fairly
recently, replacing an older, much less attractive name,
'insignificant loch'.

So far as the various animals of the hills are concerned,
foxes, deer, cattle, cats (presumably wild) and even pigs are to
be found in the Gaelic without undue difficulty. Many a
fisherman is acquainted with the little hill-loch out of which
the Lawers burn flows, Lochan a' Chait — maybe named
after some legendary wildcat of the neighbourhood; there is a
Beinn a' Chait (almost a 'Munro') in the Forest of Atholl; an
important pass through the Cluanie hills is that of the cat's
corrie, Bealach Coir' a' Chait. Not really quite so picturesque
is Meall Dearg Choire nam Muc in Ardgour, the 'lumpy hill
of the red corrie of the swine'. In Gaelic the word for 'calf' is
laogh (anglicised to *lui*) and this is found most obviously in
Beinn Laoigh (Ben Lui), although it is sometimes maintained
that in this instance the name is from *luaidhe*, meaning 'lead',
from the nearby leadmines above Tyndrum. Nowhere is there
a more apt choice than in the Cairngorms, where Lairig an
Laoigh, the 'calves' pass', leads gently south through the hills
from Nethybridge, finally reaching Deeside down Glen Lui.

The Cairngorms are indeed particularly rich in animal
references: the summit rocks of Ben Avon are known as the
'couch of the tawny stag'; at a turn of Glen Avon to the north
is Cnap an Dobhrain, the 'otter's knoll', while the steep rocks
of the 'lurcher's crag', Creag an Leth-choin, flank the 'V'-
notch of the Lairig Ghru, so familiar in the view from
Aviemore. "There is an old tradition," writes Mr Seton
Gordon, "scarcely remembered now, that a great deer
hunt — or, according to another version, a fox hunt — long
ago took place in the Cairngorms. The chase began at
Rebhoan, and ended on Creag an Leth-choin, where one of

the dogs in its eager chase fell over the black cliff that drops sheer to the Lairig below."*

Another name associated perhaps with the hunting days of old is Beinn Oss, just south of Tyndrum, in Perthshire. The Gaelic *os* may have the quite commonplace meaning of 'deer' or 'stag'; on the other hand it could equally well be translated as 'elk', which prompts the fascinating speculation that hereabouts, before the great forests of the Highlands were largely destroyed, the elk or moose was hunted until the time of its final disappearance about A.D. 1300.

Sheep are given quite an insignificant look-in in the catalogue of animals, perhaps because of their comparatively recent and tragic introduction at the time of the Clearances. By contrast, goats keep turning up with such monotonous regularity that one cannot help thinking they must have been almost embarrassingly numerous in the glens and on the high tops. The Gaelic for goat is *gabhar* or *gobhar*, with the usual puzzling combinations and permutations for plurals and genitives. Thus we have Carn nan Gabhar as the main summit of Beinn a' Ghlo, above Blair Atholl; Sgurr nan Gobhar as a spur above the 'corrie of the milkmaid' in Skye; Sgor Gaibhre between Loch Ossian and Loch Ericht; a Carn nan Gobhar on the north side as well as on the south side of Glen Strathfarrar; best known of all probably, Stob Ghabhar in the Black Mount, and many others besides. It is not really surprising, of course, that goats, like deer, should have frequent mention in the names of the hills. Herds of various sizes and often of considerable antiquity frequent many of the mountainous districts of Scotland, and although probably originally of domestic stock, are now accepted as belonging to our natural wild animals. In Galloway there have for long been herds on the slopes of The Merrick and in Glen Trool, some today possibly descendants of those that helped King Robert the Bruce to defeat the English at Moss Raploch — a victory commemorated by Bruce's Stone near Clattering-shaws Loch — by being fathered in with the horses to create the impression of a Scots army double its true size. On Ben Lomond, where a herd which is reported to have been varying

* *The Cairngorm Hills of Scotland*, by Seton Gordon (Cassell, 1925).

in numbers between forty and two hundred and fifty is to be seen, often on the shoulder known as Ptarmigan, the animals again are said to date back to Bruce's day. Only a little further north a small herd has been recorded on Beinn Chabhair and the neighbouring hills above Glen Falloch, while "about forty" goats were mentioned in 1819 by the poet Robert Southey as frequenting Ben Venue, above Loch Katrine.

It is not possible to find meanings for anything like all the hill-names that are met with; some have obviously been distorted in spelling or pronunciation out of all recognition; others are quite simply untranslatable. The experts, of course, are not always slow to put forward their theories, although sometimes these can seem so far-fetched as to be laughable; it is better, I believe, to admit defeat and leave a blank or a question mark, than to let imagination run too far out of control.

One name which most unfortunately has no certain interpretation is that of Ben Nevis. One suggestion is that it means 'sky-touching mountain'. In addition to the Ben itself we have Glen Nevis and the River Nevis, while north-westwards in Knoydart there is Loch Nevis, cutting inland from the Sound of Sleat alongside its neighbour Loch Hourn. According to tradition the latter is the 'loch of the nether regions', so that there might be some argument in favour of the theory that Loch Nevis, by way of humorous contrast, is the 'heavenly loch'. However, the contention seems rather more likely that Nevis means 'venomous' or 'malicious'; certainly those who have experienced at first hand the sheer ferocity of storm on the Ben would hardly be likely to disagree.

Now and again one comes across names which are quite exceptionally apt — names that ring emphatically true and are impossible to forget. Am Basteir, the peak next to Sgurr nan Gillean in that magnificent sweep of the Cuillin seen from Sligachan Hotel, is the 'executioner', no doubt from the outline of the sinister black rock-tooth beside it, closely resembling a headsman's axe. By way of contrast Beinn a' Bhuird, 'table mountain', looks flat enough to allow horse and rider a good half dozen miles of carefree galloping. Standing guard at the entrance to Glencoe, the two 'herdsmen' of Etive, Buachaille Etive Mor and Buachaille Etive Beag, are among the best known peaks in the Highlands and surely, too, among the most aptly named.

Sometimes old half-forgotten stories still cling to the hill-tops. The highest point of Glamaig, for example, just to the east of Sligachan, in Skye, had the local name of Sgurr Mhairi, or 'Mary's peak', after a woman who lost her life while out searching for a lost cow; was this, one wonders, on a day of bitter storm when the snow was funnelling pitilessly through Glen Sligachan from a leaden winter sky, or was it a slip on sun-scorched grass, treacherously steep above a cliff-face? On the lonely Wester Ross hill Beinn Airidh Charr, near Loch Maree, a fiercely steep tower edging the summit plateau is known locally as Martha's Peak; according to legend, Martha used to take her goats to pasture on the hills thereabouts and is reputed to have made the first traverse of the tower. Unfortunately she happened to drop her distaff — perhaps an unfair mechanical aid to the climb anyway — and in attempting to recover it fell and was killed. High above Glen Feshie, in a hollow below the summit of Carn Ban Mor, a prominent snow-bed has the name of Ciste Mhairearaid, or 'Margaret's coffin'. The tradition is that Margaret, who had been jilted by Mackintosh of Moy and had cursed his family to sterility, died here in her mad wanderings.

Some of the peaks on the main Cuillin Ridge in Skye bear the names of men now almost legendary in the annals of climbing there. Most appropriately the first of these was the highest, Sgurr Alasdair, so called after that bold and imaginative pioneer Sheriff Alexander Nicolson, who made the first ascent in 1873. Almost next to Sgurr Alasdair above the majestically wild cirque of Coire Lagan is another fine peak, Sgurr Mhic Coinnich, named after the famous guide John Mackenzie, who died in 1934; the latter's even more celebrated climbing partner, Professor Norman Collie, was commemorated by Sgurr Thormaid — a less impressive summit altogether, with little about it to interest the genuine mountaineer. Sgurr Thearlaich is named after Charles, one of the Pilkington brothers who made rock-climbing history on 18th August 1880 by proving that the Inaccessible Pinnacle of Sgurr Dearg was not impregnable after all.

Here and there among the hills remarkable natural features

have been given equally remarkable names. There is, for instance, the striking outline known as Wellington's Nose seen beyond the head of Loch Carron from the Strome by-pass, or Lord Berkeley's Seat, the airy little knob of rock which makes one of the 'tops' of An Teallach. In Arran Ceum na Caillich, the well-known 'witch's step', is the dramatic cleft in the long ridge climbing up from the east to the Castles, the second highest summit on the island. In Skye there is the famous Cioch, or 'pap', the out-thrust rock promontory which was 'discovered' by Norman Collie back in the summer of 1906 and which has since been a holiday lode-stone for the climbers of four generations. There is also, of course, a Sgor na Ciche overlooking Loch Nevis and another, the better-known Pap of Glencoe, above Loch Leven, while A'Chioch of Beinn Bhan in the Applecross hills is near neighbour to A'Chioch of Sgurr a' Chaorachain. Despite all this rivalry, however, the Skye Cioch is certainly the one most often visited. In the Cairngorms, two rock pillars on opposite sides of Loch Einich are known as Am Bodach, 'the old man', and A'Chailleach, 'the old woman'. They are apparently an unusually sporting couple, as it is said that when no one is looking they enjoy tossing a friendly boulder or two at each other across the mile-wide gap.

In Jura, according to some authorities, Beinn an Oir is the 'hill of gold', named after nearby buried treasure; in the heart of Perthshire there is a 'hill of silver', Airgiod Bheinn. And yet at the end of the day the ordinary basic 'currency' will in all probability be remembered with just as much affection as the more fancifully named such as these: the Ben Mores — so easy to pick out on the map from Cowal to Assynt and from Mull to Crianlarich; the hills with the lochans or the rough corries or the notched ridges; those which, after all, have looked red or grey, white or blue or black since long before the beginnings of history.

3
Early Days

It is entertaining, although perhaps of somewhat questionable benefit, to try to penetrate the rolling grey mists which blur and distort and hide so persistently the early story of the Scottish hills. Mythology and the supernatural provide plenty of picturesque touches, but they have a way too of adding rather noticeably to the confusion.

Just as in the Alps local peasants and travellers alike used to imagine that the snows were the haunt of dragons and demons, so those who lived in the lonely places of the Highlands had their fears and superstitions. One legendary being it was presumably best to avoid was the *glaistig*, a hag or she-devil, half human and half fairy, said to go about in the form of a goat; another was the *uruisg*, or water-demon, according to one Gaelic dictionary 'a being supposed to haunt lonely and sequestered places.' Not surprisingly, parts of the Cuillin of Skye were favourite resorts of both these strange creatures.

Legend has it that the king of the *uruisgean* had his home in Glen Lyon, even managing to leave a footprint on one of the rocks by the road-side. It was, however, in Coire nan Uruisgean, on the side of Ben Venue overlooking Loch Katrine, that the whole clan of them used to congregate, presumably to hold their annual general meetings. Sir Walter Scott refers briefly to the place in *The Lady of the Lake*:

> By many a bard, in Celtic tongue,
> Has Coir-nan-Uriskin been sung;
> A softer name the Saxons gave,
> And call'd the grot the Goblin-cave.

He was taken humorously to task nevertheless by Dr John Macculloch for attracting the tourists in droves with far too

imaginative a description of the whole Trossachs
neighbourhood — and that as long ago as 1824.*

The *each uisge*, or water-horse — as for example frequented
Loch Avon in the Cairngorms — was said to be impossible to
tame unless with a silver bridle; he would wait quietly for
some unsuspecting passer-by to try to mount him, then gallop
off into the deepest part of the loch, carrying the luckless rider
to his doom. On the other hand the *tarbh uisge*, or water-bull,
was reputedly of a kindlier disposition, usually inhabiting
smaller lochans high in the hills. Macculloch,
however — again amusingly contemporary — makes the bull
out to be a thoroughly awkward customer, as elusive as his
modern relatives in Loch Ness and Loch Morar; one imagines
he would have been an interesting witness for the Loch Ness
Phenomena Investigation Bureau:

> If I had ever seriously doubted of the Water Bull, my incredulity must
> have been demolished by once meeting a native who was watching to
> shoot one that had committed some ravages on his sheep "twenty days
> ago;" "going up and down the lake, as big as a house." An attempt had
> been made to take him, by a hook baited with a dog; but he had broken
> away, and "the lake was filled with blood." This goblin being
> invulnerable, like Claverhouse, with aught but silver shot, he had loaded
> his gun with sixpences; while his two sons were disturbing the water
> where it was concealed, with dung forks.†

Another creature of somewhat suspect likeability was the
beithir, a destructive demon which evidently had a way of
haunting caves, corries and mountain fastnesses generally and
in particular those of Beinn a' Bheithir, the well-known
horseshoe hill overlooking Ballachulish. It is not too clear all
the same precisely what damage it did cause. The Devil
himself seems to have been around quite a bit, if one judges by
the number of natural features to which he gave his name: his
Beef Tub, for instance, in the Moffat hills, or his exhilarating
Ridge which runs south from Sgurr a' Mhaim in the
Mamores. One especially picturesque effort appears to have
been when he gave a frolicsome flick of his tail as he was

The Highlands and Western Isles of Scotland, by Dr John Macculloch
(London, 1824).
  †ibid.

passing along over the north side of Auchineden Hill and sliced out the Whangie, the craggy gulch so much frequented on summer evenings by rock-climbing enthusiasts from Glasgow.

According to legend, several hills had associations with an old witch known as the Cailleach Bheur. Her chief seat is said to have been Ben Nevis and there, most inconsiderately, she used to keep a beautiful maiden prisoner. Her son, however, fell in love with the girl and in due course the young couple managed to elope, the Cailleach — without undue difficulty, one suspects — raising a succession of storms to try to keep them apart. The Cailleach is associated also with Schichallion, where she went in rather more prosaically for ploughing, the 'old wife's furrow', Sgriob na Cailleach, being apparently still discernible today. On Ben Cruachan she had a different job to do, and the story goes that she fell down on this rather badly. Every morning she had to lift aside a huge stone from a spring and every evening she had to put it back. Unfortunately, however, after a particularly arduous day's hunting she dozed off and completely neglected her evening chore of stopping up the spring. Result — Loch Awe.

It was evidently a matter of course for giants to stalk the hills long before the heyday of Am Fear Liath Mor, the Big Grey Man of Ben Macdhui. According to one folk tale, the strongest of them all lived on Ben Ledi, near Callander, proving his supremacy by beating his rivals in a challenge match at putting the stone. On the steep hill-slopes above Glencoe those mythical giants the Fingalians are said to have hunted the red deer, and it is from them that the peak of Sgor nam Fiannaidh derives its name. They seem to have moved around a fair amount, for Fingal himself is reputed to have chained his famous hunting hound Bran to the Dog's Pillar at Oban, while two of his mates, Nicol and Sguaban, preferred to while away the time in Mull with some playful boulder-lobbing at each other from Glen More to Loch Spelve across the intervening hills. Ossian's Cave, the familiar black gash high on the north face of Aonach Dubh in Glencoe, is, of course, named after the famous poet son of Fingal, but one begs leave to doubt whether the poet himself ever visited the place: the approach, by way of 'Ossian's Ladder', is a particularly

unpleasant climb up steep, vegetatious rock, and the floor of
the cave itself tilts back between dripping walls at an angle of
45° — a habitation of very questionable comfort.

It was in neighbouring Glen Etive that Deirdre, fairest of
women, lived happily with her lover Naoise. On Stob
Grianan, the 'sunny peak' at the crook of the glen, she had her
bower, roaming the hills from there as together they hunted
the red deer. The legend tells how they had only a short time
in the glen before they were lured treacherously into sailing
away with Fergus, Knight of the Red Branch, to the doom in
Ireland which Deirdre herself had foreseen.

With the earliest written records of history, a few rents and
tatters begin to appear in the clouds. We are told by the
historian Tacitus how in the year A.D. 81 his father-in-law,
the Roman general Agricola, invaded Scotland and advanced
to the line of the Forth and Clyde. Two years later his Ninth
Legion defeated the northern Picts under their chieftain
Calgacus at Mons Graupius, a battle-site not yet precisely
identified and one which there is a strong temptation to place
somewhere high in the Grampians; in fact it was almost
certainly near the Roman fort of Raedykes in comparatively
low-level country not far from Stonehaven. Thereafter the
strategy of the invaders became more defensive in intention
and Agricola was ordered to withdraw. In 121 the Emperor
Hadrian visited Britain and built his famous wall from the
Solway to the Tyne; then, a couple of decades later, Lollius
Urbicus became Governor of Britain and, pushing north once
again to the Forth-Clyde line, built the wall named after
Antonine. And here, from the windswept turf ramparts or
from the doors of their crude wooden hutments the Roman
legionaries would look still farther north, in weary boredom
maybe, to the smoky blues and the bleak winter snows of Ben
Lomond and the Campsies and the vaguer, even more
inhospitable skyline ridges beyond.

The meaning of the name Ben Lomond is uncertain,
although the most likely suggestion is that it is 'beacon hill', a
name which, incidentally, would also apply most aptly to the
commanding Lomond Hills of Fife. Firing the beacons could
be literally of life and death importance in the old days, and
serious mention is even made of it in, for example, the laws

Sgurr Dearg, Skye. The Inaccessible Pinnacle forms its summit

The wedge peak of Askival (2,659 feet), highest of the Rum hills

relating to Border warfare. In Galloway such isolated hills as Criffel and Cairnsmore of Fleet were recognised heights where the fires would be set ablaze when it was necessary to summon the men of the district to arms. So far as Ben Lomond is concerned, it certainly has a particularly commanding outlook in every direction, from Stirling and the Forth estuary in the east to the Paps of Jura in the west, from Tinto in the south to Ben Nevis in the north. Equally its own familiar lines are well seen from all round about, so that one can readily imagine the warning fires on its summit flaring out against the night sky to be seen and noted from afar: maybe by the lake-dwellers in their crannogs on Loch Lomond itself; certainly by the Roman legionaries, and by the Norsemen in their war-galleys bringing fire and sword to the islands; later, perhaps, by the watchmen in Stirling Castle in the days of Robert the Bruce.

Nowadays there is an annual pilgrimage up the well-worn path to the top of Ben Lomond to watch the sun rise on Midsummer's Day. In ancient times, however, it seems to have been Ben Ledi, 13 miles away as the crow flies, which drew the crowds year by year. This hill, apparently, was held sacred by the inhabitants of the surrounding country and on its summit the Beltane fires were lighted on 1st May in honour of the sun. According to the *Statistical Account* of 1794:

> By reason of the altitude of Ben Ledi, and of its beautiful conical figure, the people of the adjacent country, to a great distance, assembled annually on its top, about the time of the summer solstice, during the Druidical priesthood, to worship the Deity. This assembly seems to have been a provincial or synodical meeting, wherein all the different congregations within the bounds wished to get as near to heaven as they could, to pay their homage to the God of heaven. Tradition says that this devotional meeting continued three days.

It is just to be hoped that the worshippers of those days were not disappointed quite as often by low cloud and rain as are the midsummer enthusiasts of today.

Away to the north-east, a hill-climb of quite a different character dates back nearly a thousand years. The origin of the famous Braemar gathering, it is said, was in fact in the days of Malcolm Canmore, who became king of Scotland in 1057 after Macbeth, the murderer of his father King Duncan, had himself been slain. Malcolm had built a hunting seat, Kindrochit Castle, on the east side of the Clunie Water close by today's Braemar, and here he decided to stage a hill-race in order to find out which of his subjects were the best runners and potentially therefore his most useful messengers. The finish of the race was to be the top of Creag Choinnich (1,764 feet), while the first prize was to be a splendid baldric and sword, besides a purse of gold. Among the contestants were the two eldest sons of McGregor of Ballochbuie. Soon they were away and the spectators moved forward eagerly to watch their progress to the summit of the steep little hill. Suddenly yet another competitor, McGregor's youngest son, arrived breathless at the starting-point. Asking permission to compete, he was told he had now no hope, but despite this handicap, he started off in hot pursuit. Naturally, to the delight of all, he won the race in a dramatic neck-and-neck finish.

From time immemorial the Grampians have played an important part in Scotland's history. Early writers always refer to the range as the Mounth, and this designation is still to be found in some of the names of the roads and tracks leading across from Angus to Deeside — Cairn o'Mount, for example, from Fettercairn to Banchory, or Cryne Cross Mounth from Drumlithie to Crathes. This latter route is thought to have been that followed by Edward I when he led his invading forces north to Aberdeen in 1296; on his return south the probability is that the Cairn o' Mount track was used. The Cryne Cross Mounth was again of military significance three and a half centuries later when, in September 1644, Montrose chose to cross by it to Deeside after the Battle of Tippermuir.

Like the more familiar Cairnwell pass farther to the west, these Mounth roads were, of course, much used by peace-time travellers also. One crossing, from Invermark in Glen Esk to Ballater, passes close to the summit of Mount Keen (3,077 feet) and was used by John Taylor the Water Poet (he was a waterman on the Thames) in the course of his celebrated 'Pennyless Pilgrimage', thus making him one of the earliest 'Munro-baggers' on record:

> I did go through a countrey called Glaneske, where passing by the side of a hill, so steepe as the ridge of a house, where the way was rocky, and not above a yard broad in some places, so fearfull and horrid it was to

looke downe into the bottome, for if either horse or man had slipt, he had fallen (without recovery) a good mile downeright . . .

The next day I travelled over an exceeding high mountaine, called mount Skeene, where I found the valley very warme before I went up it; but when I came to the top of it, my teeth beganne to dance in my head with cold, like virginals jacks; and withall, a most familiar mist embraced me round, that I could not see thrice my length any way: withall, it yeelded so friendly a deaw, that it did moysten thorow all my clothes; where the old proverbe of a Scottish miste was verified, in wetting me to the skinne.*

The date was July 1618; the description of the weather has a not unfamiliar ring about it.

To King Robert the Bruce the hills and moors and glens of the west and south must have been thoroughly — often uncomfortably — familiar. The many skirmishes of his earlier years saw him ranging far and wide, especially in Galloway as the tide of success against the English began slowly to turn in his favour. Possibly the best known action in the south was that among the steep screes of Mulldonach, a hill near the head of Loch Trool. Hereabouts Bruce had been rallying his supporters following his landing in Carrick, when news reached him that an English force from Carlisle had made its way into Glen Trool and was uncomfortably close on his trail. Hastily his men were set to preparing an ambush. High on the hillside above the track which the enemy were expected to follow loose granite boulders were stacked in readiness; below, a rock-face dropped sheer to a deep stretch of the loch. Next morning the trap was sprung. As soon as the English were at their most vulnerable, strung out in single file across the crags, the signal was given and the rocks were prized loose in a shattering sulphurous avalanche. The result was not long in doubt. The rout was complete, those who escaped having to face the arrows of the jubilant Scots bowmen.

Then six years later, in 1313, almost on the eve of Bannockburn, comes one of the most stirring exploits in Scottish military history and, incidentally, the earliest recorded Scottish rock-climb: the capture of Edinburgh Castle

---

The Pennyless Pilgrimage, or The Moneylesse Perambulation of John Taylor, Alias, The King's Majestie's Water-Poet. Quoted extensively in *Early Travellers in Scotland*, by P. Hume Brown (Edinburgh, 1891).

by Bruce's nephew Thomas Randolph, Earl of Moray. The story is vividly told in *The Bruce*, the great epic poem written by John Barbour around the year 1375: how the Scots were laying siege to the castle when news came through that Roxburgh had been taken by a trick; how Randolph decided not to be outdone, and how he enlisted the services of a guide, a young man named William Francis who earlier had actually lived in the castle and done his courting by making nightly sallies down the rock-face to visit his girl friend in the town. The only mechanical aid which Francis recommended was a twelve-foot ladder for scaling the final wall. The night of the assault was dark and murky, so that Randolph and his thirty followers were able to climb unsuspected by the watchmen patrolling the ramparts above. Once they thought they had been discovered when a sentry tossed over a stone, but it was no more than a coincidence and they reached the wall without mishap. The climb was led by Francis, with Sir Andrew Gray second and Randolph third; then, according to a modern version of the poem,

> When those below beheld their lord
> Thus climbing up upon the wall,
> Like madmen did they follow all.

And so in due course, after a short sharp tussle inside the walls, initiative and courage met with complete triumph.

Since that black night more than six and a half centuries ago the Castle Rock has been climbed on various occasions. Now and again, of course, this means that police and fire engines have had to turn out and stand unenthusiastically by. There have, however, been less irresponsible ascents, one such having been made in May 1958. The official description of it, in the abrupt modern idiom, reads as follows:

> About 350 ft. (Severe). (1) 80 ft. — Up broken rocks and short steep column to start of obvious white shelf left of great central overhang. (2) 70 ft. — Up shelf and left to belay. (3) 50 ft. — Right by zigzags past tree to stance above overhang. (4) 120 ft. — Up overhanging corner 15 ft., then by steep grass to foot of Castle wall (no belay). (5) Up wall.*

A remarkable achievement indeed; yet surely no more remarkable than the original ascent by that party of thirty

*S.M.C.J. Vol. 26, No. 150, p. 419.

plus, in the pitch dark, without a sound and lugging a twelve-foot ladder.

Apart, however, from the one incident of the storming of Edinburgh Castle, most of the rock-climbing feats of long ago seem to have been performed quite unspectacularly; usually, in fact, in the course of the day's work.

On the Bass Rock, for example, some two miles off the East Coast at North Berwick, a wildfowler known as 'The Climber of the Bass' was employed for many years to capture gannets on the dizzy 300-foot cliffs — surely the first instance of climbing being indulged in professionally in Scotland. According to an old record of 1674, the Climber's 'bag' for that year was 1,118 gannets and these were sold for £79. 3. 10d; his own princely salary was £11. 12. 2d. Nowadays no doubt the job would have qualified for a substantial bonus of danger money, for the trap-rock slats and shelves of the Bass are notoriously steep and treacherous. Indeed, one traveller of those times, the English naturalist John Ray, records how the egg-gathering there was an occupation which killed at least one climber a year. According to Ray the young gannets were esteemed a particularly choice dish in Scotland, "and sold very dear (1s. 8d. plucked)." As recently as last century, in Queen Victoria's day, a dish of them was being sent annually as a special delicacy for the royal table.

Meanwhile off the West Coast exploits no less daring were being carried out as a matter of everyday routine on island cliffs even lonelier and more forbidding than those of the Bass — a particularly interesting fact, incidentally, in view of the recent remarkable upsurge in popularity of sea-cliffs and stacks of all kinds from Orkney to the Mull of Galloway.

In his *Description of the Western Islands of Scotland*, dated 1695, Martin Martin tells how the almost inaccessible rock of Lianamul, 369 feet high and lying off Mingulay to the south of Barra, was assaulted by the local wildfowlers. It seems to have been a thoroughly hazardous undertaking, the leader — "a big man having strength and courage proportionable" — getting the party ashore and up the rock with the help of one of the horse-hair ropes used in those days; his reward, "a few fowls more than his fellow, besides a greater esteem to compensate his courage." The rich grass covering the top of Lianamul was said to provide sufficient pasture for five sheep, and a hundred years after Martin, the author of the *Statistical Account* records how the Mingulay islanders used to hoist their animals up and down by means of a rope — a procedure which has its modern parallel on the Fair Isle headland of Sheep Craig, where good grazing above a sheer cliff-face apparently makes similar manhandling well worth while.

It was, however, on the stupendous guano-whitened cliffs of St Kilda that the old-time climbers really came into their own. The islanders there were taught almost from birth the techniques which, later, were to ensure their livelihood, and it is said that the men — stocky, muscular and sure-footed as chamois — had developed a bone-structure in their ankles which facilitated movement up and down the great rock-faces, and more widely set toes which were almost prehensile on ledge and gutter and knife-edge.

Martin himself, not surprisingly, was immensely impressed by what he saw during his own visit: "I fear it would be thought an hyperbole to relate the inaccessibleness, steepness, and height, of those formidable rocks which they venture to climb." He tells of watching some of the men following a route up one steep corner with their backs to the rock and making use only of their heels and elbows, and he describes the famous 'mistress-stone', high on a cliff-face to the south of the village, on which every suitor for a local girl had to prove his manhood by balancing on his left foot and bowing low enough to touch his toes. One of the St Kildans suggested quite seriously to Martin that he might like to have a go at this before he went home, but the offer was politely — and no doubt firmly — declined.

In those days towards the end of the seventeenth century many thousands of gannets were being taken from Boreray and its two spectacular outliers, Stac Lee and Stac an Armin. Puffins, too, were easily snared, some slight idea of the numbers involved being possible when it is realised that the harvest of one much later peak season, 1876, was reckoned at upwards of 89,000 birds. Most important of all, however, was the fulmar, which provided eggs, meat, feathers, and the oil which was so essential for lighting the cottages during the long dark nights of winter. The number of fulmars taken had fallen considerably by the time of the First World War, although as late as 1928, two years before the evacuation of St Kilda, 4,000 birds were actually preserved for eating.

Stac Lee (544 feet), with its criss-cross of ledges picked out in spring and early summer by thousands of sitting gannets, is said to be one of the most sensational outlying sea-stacks in the world; a sight of it certainly — white-ringed with bursting spray above a sea of sunlit blue — is an ingredient of any visit to St Kilda that is wholly unforgettable. Its ascent was regarded as the initiation or passing-out test for a St Kildan cliff-fowler. Also off Boreray and looking from some directions like an immense canine tooth, Stac an Armin (627 feet), with its tricky landing, tilted ledges and airy two-pronged summit, had the reputation of being more difficult than Stac Lee. A third rock-fang, Stac Biorach (236 feet), though less high, was reckoned to be the hardest climb of all and was one which only a few of the natives could lead; it rises sheer and uncompromisingly hostile from the wildly malevolent tide-jabble which separates Soay from the main island of the group, Hirta.

All these stacks have been climbed by 'outsiders' and various accounts are available for those who like exciting armchair reading. Details of the route up Stac Biorach were set down by Sir Robert Moray as long ago as 1698 and certainly lack in no way for dramatic effect:

> After they landed, a man having room for but one of his feet, he must climb up twelve or sixteen fathoms high. Then he comes to a place where having but room for his left foot and left hand, he must leap from thence to another place before him, which if he hit right the rest of the ascent is easy, and with a small cord which he carries with him he hales up a rope whereby all the rest come up. But if he misseth that footstep (as often times they do) he falls into the sea and the (boat's) company takes him in and he sits still until he is a little refreshed and then he tries it again, for everyone there is not able for that sport.

The actual climbing on St Kilda was done barefoot or else in coarse socks, while the horse-hair ropes that were used were protected by cowhide from fraying on the rocks. Noosed gins, also of horse-hair and tied to the ends of fishing-rods, were

skilfully manipulated to snare the birds. One near-tragedy
with one of these snares is vividly described by Martin:

> As he was walking barefoot along the rock where he had fixed his gin,
> he happened to put his toe in a noose, and immediately fell down the
> rock, but hung by the toe, the gin being strong enough to hold him, and
> the stones that secured it on each end being heavy. The poor man
> continued hanging thus for the space of a night, on a rock twenty
> fathoms height above the sea, until one of his neighbours, hearing him
> cry, came to his rescue, drew him up by the feet, and so saved him.

This, at least, is one kind of sea-cliff hazard which the 'hard
men' of today, constantly on the look-out for tougher and
tougher problems, never need to take too seriously.

If it was the gannets and puffins and fulmars which in the
olden days shaped the pattern of life in the outlying islands, on
the Highland mainland it was equally certainly the cattle. For
centuries the cattle population of the glens had been
considerable, the main wealth of the clans. For example, in
the middle of the sixteenth century there seems to have been
abundance everywhere, and already by that time there had
been spasmodic trading with England. The earliest traffic,
however, was mainly the wholesale raiding which took place
between glen and glen; indeed so widespread was the thieving
throughout the sixteenth and early seventeenth centuries that
it could almost have been described as the national sport.

In summer each year, after the wearying spring ploughing
on the farms, the beasts would customarily be taken to graze
high on the common hill-ground; in autumn they would be
brought down again for wintering at kindlier levels. Down the
years the pattern persisted unchanged. East and west the
story would be the same, the very fabric of life in the
Highlands. Far up those fine glens of Angus, for
instance — Glen Isla, Glen Prosen and Glen Clova — the
bullocks would be driven to the familiar grazing grounds. In
seemingly safe surroundings, as at the Shielin', under the
steep crags of Caderg, where Perthshire, Aberdeenshire and
Angus meet, they would be tended until, as the summer
passed, they became sleek and fat. But now and again,
without warning, the raiders would steal over the passes from
Deeside or Atholl and there would be bloodshed and burning
and the settling of old scores.

In some parts of the country, where the woods were thickest and most extensive, there would be excellent concealment at low levels: for example, along much of the notorious 'thieves' road', Rathad nam Mearlach, which took the caterans of Lochaber through the crowding pines of Rothiemurchus and Glenmore to the rich cattle-lands of Banff and Moray. Sometimes, on the other hand, the raiders would go high, making use of lonely passes such as the Lairig Ghru and the Lairig an Laoigh through the Cairngorms. Sometimes, too, the remote upper corries, with their burns and more often than not a secluded lochan, would be used as ideal hideouts. In Glencoe, for instance, it was to the 'corrie of capture' or 'booty', Coire Gabhail (or, as it is now more usually called, 'the lost valley'), situated 1,000 feet above the glen floor, that the Macdonalds would drive the cattle — their own or anyone else's — whenever a raid threatened. The corrie-walls there are so steep and the entrance is so narrow, that the place must have provided almost perfect concealment.

Cattle-lifting was, of course, one good reason why there was little love lost between Macdonalds and Campbells prior to the massacre of Glencoe in February 1692. Fifty years earlier the Macdonalds had formed part of Montrose's army during the whirlwind campaigning of the Civil War, and this had provided golden opportunities for plundering Campbell country. Again, in 1688, they had fought with Bonnie Dundee at Killiecrankie, returning home — once more on plunder bent — through the rich territory of Campbell of Glenlyon. Small wonder that the same Captain Robert Campbell of Glenlyon, commanding the company of Argyll's regiment which was billeted in the glen that fatal February, should have been more than ready to savour the sweet taste of revenge. It was before first light on 13th February that the massacre began, as shots were fired and the sky was reddened by the sudden flames of blazing thatch. Some thirty-eight defenceless men, women and children were killed in and around the village, but those who were able to make their escape had to face a full winter blizzard, and many more must have died of exposure as they tramped west round the shoulder of Meall Mor, or sought doubtful sanctuary in Glen Etive by way of the Lairig Gartain. Even today, in the dark woods below

Clachaig, or high maybe in some sunless recess of Bidean nam Bian, it is none too easy to escape the feeling of tragedy which has lingered down the centuries in the glen.

In its long crowded history, however, Clan Campbell has other, less warlike associations with the Scottish hills. A century before Glencoe, about the year 1590, 'Mad' Colin Campbell of Glenlyon — possibly the builder of Meggernie Castle — made the ascent of Stuchd an Lochain (3,144 feet), surely the first time on record of one of the 'Munros' being climbed. Across in Argyll, too, one annual event of which the picturesque details have come down through the centuries was a climb up into one of the north-facing corries of Ben Cruachan. About the end of the fourteenth century the first of the Macintyres crossed over from Skye in their galley with their white cow and established themselves in Glen Noe, on Loch Etive-side. There they remained for some 300 years, and it was to the Campbells that they paid their annual rent — one white calf and a midsummer snowball, obtained high up in some shaded hollow of Cruachan. However, they must have grown tired of this recurrent plod, for at the beginning of the eighteenth century they commuted the payment into money. It was an unfortunate move, for when in due time the rent was increased, the ancestral home had to be sold.

The use of snowballs as currency was not restricted to Ben Cruachan. Pennant decided there was no difficulty at all about it, as there was a handy glacier up in the 'chasms' of Ben Nevis, while Macculloch commented after his ascent of the Ben a century and a half ago:

> It is said that Cameron of Glen Nevis holds his lands by the tenure of an unfailing snowball when demanded. He is certainly not likely to fail in his rent; but as this is said in other places also, I know not if it is truth or a popular tale.*

Perhaps the idea is not really so very far-fetched, for in the *New Statistical Account* of 1845 it is noted that

> The deep clefts on the north-east side of Benevis are never without snow. For two seasons when ice failed, the snow which gathered and

The Highlands and Western Isles of Scotland, by Dr John Macculloch (London, 1824).

condensed into ice in these clefts was of great service to the salmon-curers. The country peasants with their small hardy horses carried it down in panniers on horseback.

An amusing snowball reference of quite a different kind is made by Sir Walter Scott in a note to *The Lady of the Lake*. Observing that the reproach of effeminacy was the most bitter that could be levelled at any Highlander, he describes how Sir Ewen Cameron of Lochiel, aged upwards of seventy, had been benighted on a hunting expedition somewhere in the hills and had had to bed down in the snow. To his disgust the old chief noticed that one of his grandsons, in order to make himself a little more comfortable, had rolled a large snowball and placed it below his head. "Out upon thee," he exclaimed, kicking away the frozen bolster, "art thou so effeminate as to need a pillow?"

The idea of toughness obviously inspired the old-time tradition that every chief of the Clan Campbell had to prove his manhood by setting foot on 'the cowl of The Cobbler', the airy summit rock of that hill. History does not seem to relate whether any chief actually failed the test, although the legend would account for the name 'Argyll's Eyeglass' sometimes given to the natural window through which one usually climbs in order to reach the flat roof-top above. The tradition certainly seems to belong to fiction rather than to fact, for the late Duke of Argyll, when asked, readily admitted that he had never heard tell of it. He did, however, climb The Cobbler back in the 1920s, but quite simply, he joked, because he wanted to compare the view with that from the top of Beinn Buidhe, the 'Munro' up on the moors behind the Campbell capital, Inveraray.

Another interesting and certainly authentic ascent of the very early days was that of Goat Fell, in Arran. It has been said that that indefatigable traveller Lugless Willie Lithgow reached the top in 1628, but although he gives an excellent description of the view in his remarkable book, it must surely have been at second hand, for prior to that he had been so horribly tortured in Spain as a suspected spy and in the hands of the Inquisition that climbing must have been quite out of the question. His description (presumably given him by some other, successful climber) reads:

This Ile of *Arrane* is thirty miles long, eight in breadth and distant from the Maine twenty foure Miles; being sur-clouded with *Goatfield* Hill: which with wide-eyes, over-looketh our Westerne Continent, and the Northerne Countrey of *Ireland*, bringing also to sight in a cleare Summers day, the Ile of *Manne*, and the higher Coast of *Cumberland*: A larger prospect no Mountaine in the World can show, poynting out three Kingdomes at one sight.*

For the most part, of course, the war-clouds were rarely absent for long — as in 1644 and 1645, the triumphant years of the great Marquis of Montrose, years which saw some of the most remarkable campaigning ever to have been carried out among the hills and glens of the Highlands.

In his student days at St Andrews University Montrose had earned a reputation as a particularly versatile sportsman. During his holidays, too, he seems to have been more than ordinarily energetic: on Loch Lomondside, where he often visited his sister Lilias married to Sir John Colquhoun of Luss, his steward complained that the hills of the Rossdhu estate "wore the boots off his feet." Doubtless such youthful hill-walking stood him in excellent stead for the tough campaigning of later years, the cold and the hunger and the weariness of long marches and bitter fighting.

It was in the depths of winter — in December 1644 — that Montrose, at the head of his Royalist troops, struck at his Covenanting opponents by sweeping west from Blair Atholl right to the heart of Clan Campbell country at Inveraray. Then he marched north by Loch Awe and Glencoe to face another opponent, the Earl of Seaforth. But at Kilcumin — the Fort Augustus of today — he and his 1,500 weary men were seemingly trapped: Seaforth was 30 miles ahead at Inverness with an army of 5,000; behind, at Inverlochy, were 3,000 Campbells in hot pursuit, thirsting for revenge. "Then," says John Buchan, "early on the morning of Friday, 31st January, 1645, began that flank march which is one of the great exploits in the history of British arms." Up the River Tarff towards the Corrieyairack Pass, through the snowdrifts of the Monadh Liath, and down Glen Turret and Glen Roy to the Spean the little force marched, all day and all

Travailes from Scotland to the most famous Kingdomes in Europe, Asia and Affrica (London, 1640).

night, cold and hungry and utterly weary. No doubt the scouts would be out on the surrounding moorland heights — on Glas Charn perhaps, or Beinn Iaruinn — although the enemy suspected nothing throughout the whole of that long exacting trek of more than twenty miles. On 1st February the line of advance swung farther westwards, across the winter Spean by the ford below Coire-choille, then through the Leanachan woods on the rough lower slopes of the outliers of Ben Nevis. A second night, cold and cheerless, followed. But now Inverlochy was in sight. At dawn Montrose put in his attack. The surprise was complete and in the bitter fighting which ensued the luckless Campbells — their slain almost equalling the whole of Montrose's army — were shown no shred of mercy.

Through time the rough, high-level route which Montrose and his men followed over the Corrieyairack was to form an essential part of one of the most important drove roads in Scotland. From Skye and the Western Isles and from the equally remote corners of Caithness and Sutherland the cattle came in ever growing numbers, driven south to the busy trysts at Crieff and Falkirk. Many of the herds would converge at Fort Augustus, whence, climbing to 2,543 feet at the summit of the pass, the way led on to Dalwhinnie — a muddy wisp of a trail trodden out through the heather by the hooves of countless beasts.

Not surprisingly the Corrieyairack was seen in due course as a strategic line of communication, an obvious choice for inclusion in the road-building programme of that famous soldier-engineer, Lieutenant-General George Wade.

Various steps had been taken, both before and after the Rising of 1715, to keep the peace in the troublesome North: Highland companies had been raised; forts and barracks had been built. Now — sent by King George I to investigate and report — the new 'Commander of the Forces in North Britain' saw that top priority must be given to roads and bridges. For approximately fifteen years, until he gave up his command in 1740, Wade carried through a construction programme that was to earn him lasting fame.

Although the General himself considered the ornate bridge across the Tay at Aberfeldy to be his masterpiece, he is probably better — and indeed more affectionately — remembered by the humble little humpbacks, of which he built nearly forty, and by the remarkable roads, half-forgotten now and in parts difficult to trace. The latter were planned with Roman directness, driven across bogs and peat-hags on a bottoming of boulders and trees, and taken up sharper gradients by traverses, as, for example, by the original seventeen on the Corrieyairack. Their cost was some £70 a mile.

Actual completion of the Corrieyairack road was in the late summer of 1731 and it appears to have been duly celebrated by a barbecue of roast oxen for the 500 soldiers who had worked on the job. It had been a remarkable achievement, its altitude of 2,543 feet making interesting comparison, for instance with the 2,199 feet of the Cairnwell pass between Perth and Braemar, or the 2,053 feet of the crossing to Applecross in Wester Ross over the Bealach nam Bo.

Some of the most vivid and picturesque details we have of the Highlands in Wade's day are to be found in the *Letters* which his agent and surveyor Edward Burt wrote to a friend in London. His descriptions of life in and around Inverness are particularly informative and highly diverting into the bargain. Although published in 1754, the *Letters* were actually written in 1725-26, so that Burt's account of an attempt on Ben Nevis is of outstanding interest:

> Some English Officers took it in their Fancy to go to the Top, but could not attain it for Bogs and huge perpendicular Rocks; and when they were got as high as they could go, they found a vast Change in the Quality of the Air, saw nothing but the Tops of other Mountains, and altogether a Prospect of one tremendous Heath, with here and there some Spots of Crags and Snow. This wild Expedition . . . took them up a whole Summer's Day, from five in the Morning. This is according to their own Relation. But they were fortunate in an Article of the greatest Importance to them, i.e. that the Mountain happened to be free from Clouds while they were in it, which is a Thing not very common in that dabbled Part of the Island, the Western Hills; — I say, if those condensed Vapours had passed while they were at any considerable Height, and had continued, there would have been no means left for them to find their Way down, and they must have perished with Cold, Wet, and Hunger.*

It is more than a little ironical that General Wade's

*Letters from a Gentleman in the North of Scotland (London, 1754).

roads — built, in his own words, "for the better Communication of his Majesty's Troops" — should have played an important part in the moves and counter-moves of the Forty-five. Prince Charlie used the Corrieyairack at the end of August 1745 for his crossing of the Monadh Liath from Invergarry to Dalwhinnie, hoping to bring General Cope's army to a decisive engagement in this mountain terrain so suited to his Jacobite troops. The English commander, however, was not to be drawn and side-stepped shrewdly to Ruthven barracks, near Kingussie, while the Prince marched on south, unopposed, to Perth.

Numerous accounts are extant describing at first hand the terrors of the Corrieyairack. One traveller by the name of Skrine, who crossed the pass in a carriage, found it an "inexpressibly arduous road . . . springing sometimes from point to point over alpine bridges and at other times pursuing narrow ridges of rock frightfully impending over tremendous precipices." Another writer describes it as impassable in the depths of winter, with the steep descent on the south side "particularly dangerous not only from deep snows concealing the unbeaten track of the road, but from whirlwinds and eddies that drive the snow into heaps." A young man who tackled it on horseback thought that he and his horse were going to be carried away, "so strong was the blast, so hard the rain, and so very thick the mist."

The pass appears to have remained in quite extensive use until the second half of last century. But gradually throughout the Highlands cattle had been giving way to sheep, and on the Corrieyairack, as elsewhere, the days of the drovers were numbered. Now even the driven flocks of sheep have become a distant memory and the old track over the pass is today no more than a supremely pleasant hill-walk.

In the first half of the eighteenth century the hills of Inverness-shire — and, fractionally, of Wester Ross — were very much a part of the whole bitter story of the Jacobites. Rock and heather, ridge and corrie provided a setting which, however romanticised it was to be in later years, must at the time have been harsh and tough and utterly uncompromising.

On the north side of Glen Shiel, down from Cluanie Inn and just across the county boundary into Ross-shire, is the 'peak of the Spaniards', Sgurr nan Spainteach (3,129 feet). The name, intriguingly unusual, commemorates the skirmish which took place in the glen one long June day in 1719. Three hundred Spaniards had been brought over in two frigates from San Sebastian and landed near the head of Loch Duich to join up with a larger company of Jacobite clansmen under the Earl of Seaforth; against them, from Inverness, marched a body of regular troops under General Wightman. The battle, however, seems to have been half-hearted and inconclusive, if anything going against the Jacobites and ending in the surrender of the unfortunate Spaniards. It was later described by Sir Walter Scott as "the last faint sparkle of the Great Rebellion of 1715." Twenty-seven years later Prince Charles Edward Stuart was to find himself a fugitive in that same glen, a price of £30,000 on his head. For all of a grilling summer's day he lay up behind the big boulder — 'Prince Charlie's Stone' — a mile or so east of the farm of Achnangart.

By the time that he made his final getaway to France aboard the ship *L'Heureux* in September 1746, the Prince must have been a thoroughly hardened mountaineer. The picture one is inclined to have of him — immaculate kilt, braided blue doublet, powdered wig, starched lace ruffles — must have been remarkably far from actuality. Thirteen gruelling months had elapsed since the raising of his standard at Glenfinnan; five since the blood-bath of Culloden. On sailing day it would be a deal nearer the truth to imagine a young man travel-stained, weatherbeaten, thin, and weary to the very marrow of his bones.

During the twenty-two weeks of his wandering after Culloden the Prince had come to know a bewildering variety of hideouts in the lonely places of the hills: MacEachine's refuge high in the corrie north of Loch Eilt; the hillside bivouac between Loch Cluanie and Glen Affric — a night of pouring rain in a position so precarious that he and his companions could not even lie down for some sleep; the cave with the Seven Men of Glen Moriston, devoted followers who had fought for him at Culloden; Cluny's Cage, that remarkable sanctuary fashioned out of wood and moss in a great sea of boulders high on a spur of Ben Alder. He had followed more ridges and skulked past more summits than

Ben Lomond and Loch Lomond from above Glen Douglas

A routine climb for the St Kildan wildfowlers.
Stac Lee and its sitting gannets

we know about now, sometimes so close to the enemy's camp-fires that he and his friends could hear the soldiers talking. He had crossed the summit of Fraoch-bheinn (2,489 feet), overlooking Glenfinnan; he had found Meall an Spardain (1,804 feet) an invaluable look-out point at the head of Loch Quoich; he probably used the well-known 'Window', 3,200 feet up, to cross the north-east ridge of Creag Meaghaidh. He had been sea-sick, sun-scorched, drenched to the skin; he had been lashed by gales and devoured by midges; he had known innumerable hasty departures in mist or by starlight among some of the loneliest, roughest glens and corries of the Highlands. Surely one of the most incredible escape stories in history.

4

The Heights of The Hills

There's Cairnsmore of Fleet,
  And there's Cairnsmore of Dee;
But Cairnsmore of Carsphairn's
  The highest of the three.

So runs the old Galloway rhyme; entertaining indeed, but not particularly helpful by way of accurate measurement.

Nevertheless interest in the heights of the hills was being taken not too long after the start of the eighteenth century. For example, General Wade's agent and surveyor Edward Burt, in one of the letters which he wrote from Inverness in the years 1725-26, makes interesting reference to Ben Nevis:

> As a Specimen of the Height of those Mountains, I shall here take notice of one in Lochaber, called Ben-Nevis, which, from the Level below to that Part of the Summit only which appears to View, has been several times measured by different Artists, and found to be three-Quarters of a Mile of perpendicular Height.*

Which, unless my arithmetic is at fault, makes the Ben 3,960 feet — not so very far short of the accepted 4,406 feet.

Twenty years later, at the time of the Forty-five, there were still no reliable maps of the Highlands in existence. The campaign which ended in the blood-bath of Culloden must have had plenty of topographical problems for 'Butcher' Cumberland and his staff, as indeed must also the Prince's subsequent flight through the heather. It is little wonder that Cumberland's Deputy Quartermaster General, Lieutenant-General Watson, declared it was high time to set about remedying this state of affairs and decided in fact that a map of the Highlands should be made. A special detachment of infantry was, therefore, posted to Fort Augustus in 1747 and spent the next eight years on the survey.

Largely responsible for the actual production of the map was a promising young engineer — it is not certain if he actually held any military rank at that time — by the name of

Letters from a Gentleman in the North of Scotland (London, 1754).

William Roy. Roy was then only twenty-one — he had been born at Carluke, in Lanarkshire, in 1726 — but already he was obviously thoroughly competent and looked for exceedingly high standards. In the end the map was not entirely to his satisfaction. As he himself wrote later:

> Although this work, which is still in manuscript, and in an unfinished state, possessed considerable merit, and perfectly answered the purpose for which it was originally intended; yet having been carried out with instruments of the common, or even inferior kind, and the sum allowed for it being inadequate to the execution of so great a design in the best manner, it is rather to be considered as a magnificent military sketch, than a very accurate map of the country.

It was nevertheless a very fine piece of work and the original field sheets, for which the roads and some of the streams had been paced and the hills put in roughly by eye, have been preserved in the King's Library of the British Museum. The scale was intended to be 1,000 yards to one inch (between the 6-inch and the 1-inch scale) and although the map was never printed, it was later reduced by Roy to a single sheet and engraved for ultimate publication in his celebrated book, *The Military Antiquities of the Romans in North Britain*.

Roy received a commission in the 53rd Foot in 1756 and quickly earned promotion, becoming Surveyor-General of Coasts and Engineer for making and directing Military Surveys in Great Britain nine years later. Whenever the occasion permitted he advocated the formal establishment of a National Survey, and it is generally recognized that it was largely due to him that the Ordnance Survey was founded in 1791, the year after his death. Although his duties took him all over Britain, he never lost his close associations with Scotland and he must have been particularly interested in the work of a party of astronomers who, in 1769, chose the summit of Ben More, Crianlarich, to observe the transit of Venus. Again, in 1774, when the Astronomer Royal, the Rev. Nevil Maskelyne, spent four months on Schichallion making observations relating to the density of the earth, Roy visited him and corresponded with him about the work. In a letter to a colleague dated 26th July 1774 he remarks: "I took my leave of Maskelyne on the 15th, but I did not quit Strath Tay till the 18th, having some observations Geometrical as well as

Barometrical to make on the neighbouring Mountains." Four years later we hear of him reading a paper before the Royal Society, of which he had previously been elected a Fellow, on "Rules for Measuring Heights with a Barometer." At the same time another Fellow of the Royal Society, Dr Charles Hutton, who had been computing the results of the Schichallion experiments, appears to have been the first to hit upon the idea of using contour lines.

As an incidental footnote to the Maskelyne story it may be mentioned that in 1974, the bicentenary year of the observations, the Clan Donnachaidh (the Robertsons and their affiliated septs) had a particularly interesting exhibit on display in their Clan Museum at Bruar Falls near Blair Atholl. This was the fiddle which the Astronomer Royal, Professor Maskelyne, presented as a gift to a Rannoch boy, Ian Ruadh Drobhair, who was an entertainer for the scientific party while they were staying in their hut on Schichallion. A Gaelic song was composed on the fiddle, the title of it being 'The Yellow London Lady'.

All this scientific activity in the later years of the eighteenth century must have made for an immense amount of interest, although not everyone, even among travellers, showed much enthusiasm for the actual heights of the hills. Dr Johnson, poor fellow, was not at all impressed as he and Boswell proceeded up Glen Moriston:

> Of the hills, which our journey offered to the view on either side, we did not take the height, nor did we see any that astonished us with their loftiness.*

On the other hand, Thomas Pennant in 1769 was only fifty-six feet out with the height of Ben Nevis, and in 1772, on his Second Tour, only forty-eight feet out with Ben Lomond. Pennant was certainly a little before his time, yet within a very few years and before the eighteenth century was out, the heights of many of the hills were widely — if not altogether accurately — known. Thus the first *Statistical Account*, compiled between 1791 and 1798 by the various parish ministers, makes mention of quite a number of heights, and presumably these would be taken as true figures by the writers of the day.

A Journey to the Western Islands of Scotland (London, 1773).

For the next thirty-three years after its official constitution, the Ordnance Survey had for its object the production of a one-inch map of Great Britain. First to appear was the map of Kent, published on 1st January 1801, while during the years 1800 to 1809 the heights of some 300 hills in England and Wales were calculated with very fair accuracy. The rigours which these latter observations involved may not have been quite so severe as those experienced in the Highlands, but in Cumberland at least they provided William Wordsworth with some meat for his poem written, for some reason best known to himself, "with a slate pencil on a stone, on the side of the mountain of Black Comb":

> Know, . . .
> That on the summit whither thou art bound,
> A geographic Labourer pitched his tent,
> With books supplied and instruments of art,
> To measure height and distance; lonely task,
> Week after week pursued!

In 1810, the year in which the triangulation was pushed on into Scotland, some extraordinarily accurate barometric measurements were made in the Cairngorms by the Rev. George Skene Keith, D.D. He visited the principal summits and reckoned that Ben Macdhui (4,296 feet) was 4,300 feet high, Cairn Toul (4,241 feet) was 4,285 feet and Braeriach (4,248 feet) was 4,280 feet. In addition, he sent his son to Fort William to climb Ben Nevis with his barometer, with the result that Ben Macdhui lost the pride of place it had held until then. Fortunately a retaliatory project to build a burial vault 100 feet high at the top of Ben Macdhui failed to materialise.

During the early years of the Survey in Scotland probably the most colourful figure was the great Thomas Colby, an employee for forty-four years and Director General from 1820 until his retirement in 1846. Colby had lost a hand in a pistol accident when quite a young man, but this most certainly did not deter him from displaying a toughness and an energy which left his subordinates trailing far behind. An account, written in 1852 by a Major R.K. Dawson, of a season spent under Colby's command in the Highlands, gives an excellent picture of the latter's manner of life when at work, before he actually became Director of the Survey:

> We were joined at Huntley by Captain Colby, he having travelled through from London on the mail coach. This was Captain Colby's usual mode of travelling, neither rain nor snow, nor any degree of severity in the weather, would induce him to take an inside seat or to tie a shawl round his throat; but, muffled in a thick box-coat, and with his servant Frazer, an old artilleryman, by his side, he would pursue his journey for days and nights together, with but little refreshment, and that of the plainest kind — commonly only meat and bread, with tea or a glass of beer.
>
> From Huntley, Captain Colby proceeded with us on foot, and on the second afternoon we reached the base of the mountain [Corryhabbie, 2,563 feet] in Glen Fiddick, near to a hunting lodge of the Duke of Gordon. Here, by partially reducing the loads on the cars, and by the application of guy-ropes to support them, and with the men's shoulders to the wheels, we climbed up as far as we could; and, having unloaded the cars, made an irregular kind of encampment for the night. It was a fine evening; and we had need, therefore, of but slight covering; and anything like luxury was, of course, out of the question. A marquee was pitched for Captain Colby, in which he slept, in his clothes, on a bundle of tent-linings.
>
> On the following morning the really laborious part of the business commenced, that of conveying the camp-equippage, instruments, and stores to the top of the mountain. Horses were hired for the purpose and made to carry the packages slung like panniers over their backs, so far as the ground proved tolerably even and firm; but when it became broken and hummocky, which is commonly the case with peaty soils, or springy and wet, there was then no alternative but to unload the horses and carry the things on the men's shoulders. Captain Colby went on, taking Robe and myself with him, to the summit, where he selected a spot of ground for the encampment as near as practicable to the station, and also for the watch-tent, at a point much nearer still. He then selected a suitable place for a turf-hovel, to be built on the sloping face of the hill, with a tarpaulin roof, in which to make a fire for cooking, and for drying the men's shoes and clothes, and to serve also as a place of shelter and warmth for the men in tempestuous and severe weather. The requisite steps were then taken for securing the table or stand, for the great theodolite; and the theodolite itself was then brought up with special care and fixed in its position.
>
> When the arrangements in the observatory had been completed, and the summit of the hill was free from clouds, every moment favourable for observation was anxiously caught by Captain Colby, and devoted to that service, from sunrise to sunset.

Towards the end of June that year and during July, Colby took a small party of men on a 'station hunt', exploring the country and erecting trig points, or 'objects' as he called them, on some of the principal hills. On the first expedition they covered all the eastern side of Inverness-shire, Ross-shire and Caithness, as well as the mainland of Orkney, walking 513 miles in twenty-two days; then, after a single rest day, Colby led a fresh party westwards and north-westwards, this time walking 586 miles in twenty-two days.

The observations with the great theodolite were completed just before the end of September, and all joined in a mammoth celebration feast:

> The chief dish on such occasions was an enormous plum-pudding, the approved proportions of the ingredients being — a pound of raisins, a pound of currants, a pound of suet etc. to each pound of flour; these quantities were all multiplied by the number of mouths in camp, and the result was a pudding of nearly a hundred pounds weight.

The pudding was suspended by a cord from a cross-beam and boiled for twenty-four hours in a brewing-copper; then a long table was spread, Colby and his staff joined the men, and after the pudding had been voted excellent, a toast was drunk: 'Success to the Trig.'

In 1852 the Great Triangulation of the United Kingdom was completed. If ever celebrations were justly deserved, surely it was then, after the long years of almost incredible toil and trouble. For imagination fails to picture in any way adequately the achievements of pioneers like Roy and Colby, with their inexhaustible patience and sheer dogged determination; or of the many men, humble and unstoried, who made the whole thing possible, back-packing mountainous loads over heartbreaking country often in the most hostile weather. It is a story which is all too little known.

One Scottish hill which still had a part in the closing stages of the work was Ben Lawers, with a party of Royal Engineers encamped at the summit for several months during the summer. What memorable views they must have had! In every direction linked by direct sights to a whole circle of other outstanding peaks: to Ben Nevis and Ben Macdhui, eastwards to Glas Maol above Glen Isla, southwards to Hart Fell and The Merrick, then out to the Western Isles, to Beinn an Oir in Jura and Ben More in Mull. These were, of course, the rewards which compensated for the many blank days, the days of mist and sleet and driving rain spent huddled in cold discomfort under canvas with rude protecting walls of turf and stone. Traces of these old hill-top shelters are still sometimes to be seen and indeed as recently as 1972, while an Ordnance Survey team was at work in Ardgour, some 'remains' close to the 2,800-foot trig point on Creach Bheinn were investigated as being of archaeological interest, only to be identified as shelter walls put up by the team's predecessors more than a century ago.

During the years following the completion of the Great Triangulation the heights of the hills became comparatively widely known and accepted. Baddeley's Guide, for instance, gave a list of thirty-one summits of over 3,000 feet in height — an interesting if rather obvious selection — and any diligent seeker could easily have found more on the maps, had he felt so inclined. It was not, however, until the 'Munro era' dawned that any real interest was awakened and hill-walkers suddenly became alive to the immense possibilities for enjoyment that existed in seeking out all the most remote corners of the Highlands.

Who then was Munro, the man who was responsible for it all, the man whose name has for so long now attached to all the separate 3,000-foot mountains in Scotland?

Sir Hugh Munro, Bart, hailed from Angus, from not far from Kirriemuir. He was one of the original members of the Scottish Mountaineering Club and was indeed such an enthusiast that he may well have set up a record for attendance at the early meets of the Club. He became the third president, holding office from 1894 to 1897, and did an immense amount for the Club during the first quarter-century of its existence. In addition he was a regular contributor to the *Journal* and it was in the sixth issue — that for September 1891 — that his famous *Tables giving all the Scottish Mountains exceeding 3,000 feet in height* appeared. It was Sir Hugh's own ambition to climb them all. In the end, however, he failed narrowly, by two — the most difficult, the Inaccessible Pinnacle of Sgurr Dearg, in Skye, which defeated him several times, and one of the easiest, Carn Cloich-mhuillin, in the Cairngorms, which he was keeping for the last one, to be duly celebrated with some of his Aberdeen friends. His last attempts on the Inaccessible Pinnacle were made in

September 1915. Not long afterwards, in the spring of 1919, he died from pneumonia at the age of sixty-three.

In his original *Tables* Sir Hugh set out details of 283 separate 3,000-foot mountains, an altogether revolutionary advance on any previously published list. However, with the O.S. maps under constant revision, the heights of the hills have always been subject to a certain amount of alteration; furthermore, in the early days of the S.M.C., there was much friendly controversy as to which summits should be considered separate mountains and which merely 'tops'. In due course therefore, for the 1921 edition, Sir Hugh's list was pruned to 276, a figure which remained sacrosanct until 1974. One major omission from the first, extraordinarily accurate list had been Beinn Tarsuinn, a fine hill in the wild country to the north of Loch Maree and which had seemingly been missed by the Ordnance Survey. At Easter 1928 the conclusion was reached that the height of this peak was in fact about 3,080 feet and it was argued in consequence that it had an irrefutable claim to inclusion in the 'peerage'. And so for the 1953 edition of the *Tables* Beinn Tarsuinn was actually listed, despite the fact that it was a thoroughly awkward intruder, as it were, since it was felt it could not be given a place in the order of precedence. For all that it added one more touch of character to a list which over the years had become a classic.

It was another president of the S.M.C., the Rev. A.E. Robertson, who was the first to accomplish the feat of doing all the 'Munros' of his day. The task occupied eleven years and must have been a formidable one in days when roads were appalling by modern standards, and bicycles were the only helpful form of transport. On many of his expeditions Robertson was accompanied by his close friend Sandy (later Lord) Moncrieff, and it was with him and Mrs Robertson that the great work was duly completed in September 1901 with the ascent of Meall Dearg (3,118 feet) at the eastern end of the Aonach Eagach ridge in Glencoe. A "horrible loose scree gully" took them to the crest of the ridge, after which they walked westwards to the summit, where they duly broached the ceremonial champagne. "Sandy", wrote Robertson afterwards, "made me first kiss the cairn and then my wife!

We inserted a card with our names and the special event into the now empty bottle, which we carefully packed away among the stones of the cairn. This bottle, intact, was still there in 1930. . . . We descended the steep scree gully with ease! I, at any rate, never descended a scree slope with less trouble!'"*

It is interesting to note that the feat was not repeated for another twenty-two years and that up until the start of the Second World War no more than eight successes had been recorded. Then, in 1947, the avalanche started; soon it had assumed quite alarming proportions. There were those who added the subsidiary 'tops' — then, all 268 of them — to their list; those who claimed in addition all the three-thousanders in the British Isles outwith Scotland; some did the round twice — one at any rate three times; women and schoolboys joined the elect. By 1970 the list had topped the century. The record had it that there was even a dog which had done the lot, although there appeared to be no truth in the rumour that it was starting a separate list for its canine friends.

Much has been written, of course, on the subject of that dread disease known as 'Munromania'. The first symptoms of this generally manifest themselves as a furtive ticking off of the summits and 'tops' of the *Tables*. This is followed, much more seriously, by a compulsive desire to visit the most obscure summits, be they the dullest, flattest lumps imaginable, while many a fine peak that has been previously climbed remains tragically neglected. So far there is no known cure. On the other hand there is so much to be said in favour of 'Munro-bagging' that the argument is not really too one-sided. Above all it teaches one more about the geography of Scotland than any other pastime could possibly do and takes one to lonely, little-known parts which otherwise would never be visited.

Everything, therefore, looked serene and orderly as the august company grew steadily in numbers. Then in 1974 a further revised edition of the *Tables* made unexpected, startling history: two new 'Munros' had been 'discovered' on the latest O.S. sheets. These are Ruadh-Stac Mor and Beinn a' Chlaidheimh, both in that particularly remote area to the north of Loch Maree where Beinn Tarsuinn had already proved so awkward. All three of these peaks now find their rightful places in the order of precedence, thus making the official total of separate mountains 279. As well as this, sundry additions and subtractions have been made to the 'tops' so that that total is now six less than it was at 262. It is not yet clear what the reactions will be to this intriguing bombshell, what it will mean for all those dedicated 'Munroists' now taking their well-earned rest by the fireside. No doubt they will be reaching for boots and ice-axe to meet the fresh challenge, and sharpening pencils to be ready to place two triumphant ticks against the new names on the list. As has already been observed, there is no known cure for the disease.

It was inevitable of course that, following Munro, a further list — of all the separate 2,500-foot mountains — should have been compiled. In order to keep this within reasonable limits, a qualification of a "re-ascent of 500 feet on all sides" was strictly applied by the compiler, the late J. Rooke Corbett. As a result a total of 219 was reached (now reduced by the promotion of Ruadh-Stac Mor and Beinn a' Chlaidheimh). This included many particularly fine peaks — Goat Fell and Cir Mhor in Arran, The Cobbler, Ben Ledi, the hills of Jura and Rum, Fuar Tholl at Achnashellach, Suilven and Ben Loyal in Sutherland, to name but a few.

Two or three of these 'Corbetts' come very close to the magic 3,000-foot boundary line, several within less than ten feet of it. No one, however, seems to have come forward with a proposal to build a cairn on any of these 'near misses' in order to allow them promotion. Perhaps the effort on Ben Lawers just almost a century ago was a sufficiently telling lesson.

In *The Scottish Tourist*, published in 1825, the height of Ben Lawers is given as 4,015 feet, while in his book of the previous year on the Highlands Dr Macculloch observes that "it is supposed to exceed 4,000 feet."* This must therefore have been the accepted figure of the day, probably that calculated by Roy in 1774. However, in the Great Triangulation of 1852 Ben Lawers was demoted from its proud position among the four-thousanders and accorded its correct, present-day height of 3,984 feet. This appears to have been a source of some

---

*The Highlands and Western Isles of Scotland (London, 1824).

annoyance to a native of the district by the name of Malcolm Ferguson, for in 1878 he decided to pay for the erection of a massive cairn on the summit which would bring back the measurement above the exalted level. On 4th July about thirty volunteers from the neighbourhood set about the task and built the cairn in a day — some forty-five to fifty feet in circumference and twenty feet in height, with a white quartz cope-stone weighing nearly seven hundredweight. Thereafter each worker was rewarded for his toil with a "handsome volume of Gaelic poetry"! It was hoped that the massive structure would last for many years, but even by 1898 it had already fallen into a state of collapse and today few significant traces of the old cairn remain.

With the country now in the uncomfortable throes of going metric, it would seem that those who have always been used to the heights of our hills in feet are having to watch their world crumble in ruins about them. It is almost painful, for example, to think of Ben Nevis, its 4,406 feet familiar since earliest schooldays, transformed to a soulless 1342.06 metres; only with a shudder is it possible to contemplate Ben Lomond's well-known 3,192 feet suffering the indignity of sinking to 972.28m. Almost at a stroke the present élite of the seven four-thousanders could be said to be disappearing into outer darkness; Aonach Mor, near neighbour of Ben Nevis, is in danger of losing for ever the distinction of its 3,999 feet, Liathach its easily remembered 3,456 feet. What satisfaction, one wonders, could future generations of hill-walkers possibly hope to find in solemnly ticking off lists of paltry 914-metre summits?

Fortunately, for the present at least, the *Tables* are retained in their old form, except that they have both 6-inch and 1-inch O.S. heights included (as these, with up-dating, tend to differ) and also have the metric equivalents added. They will — one hopes — continue to be handed down to posterity as the major classic they are, although as the various O.S. sheets are modernised, so there are bound to be further changes. Like the Flying Dutchman, the 'Munroist' of the future will never know the meaning of rest.

For several years now metrication has in fact been having a profound influence on the work of the Ordnance Survey. The old era of chains and links, and rods, poles or perches belongs well and truly to the past.

The present gigantic task of re-surveying the whole of Britain — expected to be completed by 1980 — is in fact being carried out at three basic scales: 1/10,000 (replacing the old, familiar six inches to the mile), 1/2,500 (the 25-inch) and 1/1,250 (the 50-inch). The last of these is being used for the cities and larger burghs and, so far as Scotland is concerned, has now been mostly completed. In the Highlands the mountains and moorlands are being surveyed at 1/10,000, with any small towns, villages and areas of pasture-land faring better at the larger 1/2,500 scale.

Basically nowadays, the surveying depends on aerial photography. This sounds delightfully simple — at first. In fact it must be beset with uncertainty from start to finish. On average just sixteen days in a year are available for useful photography at the essential high-level heights above 10,000 feet. Moreover, in Scotland the flying season lasts only from 1st April usually until the end of September, and even during that time, if the sun is low and casting awkwardly long shadows, worth-while photography is out of the question.

The aerial film goes to headquarters at Southampton for processing and printing on glass plates, which are used by photogrammetry experts to provide an accurate network of control points. These latter enable the air surveyors, using special plotting machines, to plot with precision all the detail that can be positively identified. Contours are also surveyed and plotted in this way: a most intricate process. The whole work, from flying the photography to actual field completion on the ground, covers a period of about four years.

Helicopters, of course, have been in full use by the O.S. since about 1964. Prior to that they had been doing some useful transporting of heavy materials, mainly for some of the more remote concrete 'trig point' pillars. Now they have a dual function: airlifting the surveyors hither and yonder off the roads, as required, and making it immeasurably easier than in the past for rough country to be quickly and accurately classified. The helicopter season extends normally from Easter until the end of July and during this time each surveyor in a team has the chance of hovering over the particular map-section for which he is responsible so as to classify the ground — whether heath, woodland, outcrop rock and so on — and also to note any points at which he may need to do some detailing. Usually the helicopter flies at about 500 feet, while it has a maximum cruising time of two and a half hours. A surveyor should be able to do all the necessary recce flying in anything from half-an-hour to the full two hours.

In addition there are all the essential airlifts to strategic points near or far. Usually these work out highly satisfactorily — and are sufficiently labour-saving to make even a purist hill-walker slightly green with envy. Occasionally, however, the weather has a way of clamping down and then the luckless 'castaway' has to step it out for home. The walk-out route has always been agreed beforehand and road transport comes as far as possible, but — just in case — emergency rations, first-aid kit and distress flares are carried as a matter of routine.

Several reasons can be given for the various height revisions that have been made. For one thing, obviously, modern instruments and survey methods are much more accurate than those of the past; for another, a new triangulation pillar may not coincide exactly with the previously heighted point; yet again, because of local obstructions, pillars sometimes have to be built on cairns in order to increase visibility. Yet so precise have been recent measurements that in 1965 Major-General A.H. Dowson, then Director General of the Ordnance Survey, was able to write: "The determination of these heights has been made to a high standard of accuracy, and we believe that the new heights are correct to plus or minus 1 foot in terms of absolute altitude above our national levelling datum, established from long-term observations of mean sea level at Newlyn in Cornwall."*

Changes in familiar heights are not, of course, at all popular — with others as well as mountaineers. And so, as General Dowson added: "Every case is carefully examined before a decision is made and if our records show any ambiguity a ground inspection is usually made to determine the best height to show for the peak concerned. We

*S.M.C.J. Vol. 28, No. 157, pp. 206-7.

particularly endeavour to avoid changing the height shown on well-known peaks unless the validity of this change can be established."*

No doubt with metrication the troubles will vanish like mist from the high tops, and future generations will smile at our molehill worries. Yet a final word may fairly be added. Times and methods may have changed since the brave days of General William Roy; but one thing most obviously does not change — the high standards which keep producing the finest large-scale maps in the world.

*ibid.

5
The Tourists Arrive

Countless thousands of motorists, hurrying on their way between Loch Long and Loch Fyne, use the kindly-graded road over 'Rest and Be Thankful'. Yet there must be relatively few of them who ever pause and give thought to the older road beside it, climbing so steeply and so enjoyably up Glen Croe and reaching the summit of the pass, almost as if with a flourish of triumph, in a spectacular hairpin bend. This in early days was approximately the line of the track followed by much of the droving traffic from farther south and west in Argyll. It then became part of the fine new military road from Dumbarton to Inveraray which General Cope, who had taken over command of the Government troops in Scotland after General Wade and General Clayton, ordered to be put in hand in 1744 at an estimated cost of £4,258. The men of Lascelles' regiment were given the job, only to be called away a year later for the emergency of the Forty-five; thereafter, however, Major Caulfield and his soldiers, 800 of them, were back to resume where Cope had left off, working in conditions so uncomfortable that the men had to be kept from deserting by the inducement of a bonus of an extra sixpence a day.

Glen Croe and its hills were to be described not many years later by all the famous tourists who passed that way to or from Inveraray. Thomas Pennant and Dr Johnson, Thomas Newte and John Stoddart, Dorothy Wordsworth and the rest, all without exception were moved to the most eloquent descriptions, usually thoroughly exaggerated and almost always emphasising the gloom and the melancholy and the fearsome aspect of the surrounding crags.

It is rather pleasant all the same to let the imagination wander a little and picture some young soldier, perhaps with a companion or two, making use of a spell of leisure to explore the neighbouring hills. After all, the grass and rock slopes of Beinn an Lochain rise not much more than 2,000 feet above the top of 'The Rest' and nearby Loch Restil, and they must often have looked tempting enough of a fine summer's

On the summit rock of The Cobbler

Schichallion from the north side of Loch Rannoch

evening; Beinn Ime, too, or Beinn Donich could easily have earned reputations for their far views, and surely on occasion good sport was had on the summit rock of The Cobbler. Is it really too far-fetched to think that even in those days hills could be climbed purely for the sake of enjoyment?

Very different in motive from such imaginary carefree wanderings over the Arrochar 'Alps' were the annual pilgrimages made by a young man named James McIntyre. McIntyre had fought at the battle of Culloden, carrying the colours of John Roy, colonel of the Edinburgh regiment. With great bravery he managed to preserve the precious standard throughout the fighting, although it was "holed with balls and hacked by swords", and later he even contrived to save it from the ultimate indignity of being burnt in Edinburgh by the common hangman. Instead he cherished it dearly and once every year, on the anniversary of the raising of Prince Charlie's standard at Glenfinnan, he used to carry it to the top of Cairn Gorm and there solemnly and proudly unfurl it. He wished, he said, "to give it fresh air." Eventually the famous old flag, "dim and faded with age", passed into the keeping of the Duke of Gordon.*

Clearly, however, with the country more settled, the first desultory beginnings of the tourist 'invasion' were not to be long delayed. Thus, on 5th July 1758, a young man by the name of William Burrell set off from London for a tour of Scotland. In due course he reached Luss, and from there with some friends mounted an assault on Ben Lomond. In the neat, closely written pages of his diary, now in the National Library of Scotland, one can read:

> On the opposite side [of Loch Lomond] stands a mountain of the same name of a prodigious height, overshadowing all the neighbouring rocks; the way to it is very irksome and in some places so steep that we were obliged to crawl on hands and knees. From the beginning of the ascent to the summit is five English miles; in several parts we sunk up to our knees in mire; we were fortunate enough to have a fine day.

A farmer working at his harvest near-by, whom Burrell calls the Laird of Blairvochy, had treated the party to sour milk and

---

*In the Shadow of Cairngorm, by the Rev. W. Forsyth, M.A., D.D. (Inverness, 1900).

goat's whey. In addition he provided Burrell with a pony

which took him as far as the steep upper slopes. There he had to dismount and does not seem to have managed very much farther on foot.

> When I got within 100 yards of the top, I had the misfortune to be seized with a dizziness which prevented my Quixotism being carryed to so great a height as my friends, who feasted very heartily on the summit, whilst I was descending with the utmost caution, or rather creeping down on all fours; having returned safely with assistance to the first resting-place and refreshed myself with the relicks of their repast, we all set out together and by bogtrotting with great rapidity arrived at our hospitable laird's without any other accident, except being much dirted.

One wonders what Burrell would have thought had he been able to look into the future and see just how busy the path to Ben Lomond's summit can be nowadays on a warm summer's day.

For the most part the early travellers seem, like William Burrell, to have played up their exploits to the full. In strong contrast to this, however, are the matter-of-fact entries in the diary of James Robertson, a botanist sent out from Edinburgh in April 1767 "to examine the vegetable productions of several counties." By mid-May we find Robertson up in the far north, roaming over several hills almost as if without noticing them: Scaraben (2,054 feet) and Morven (2,313 feet) in Caithness, then down to Ben Wyvis (3,429 feet), on which he was "whitened by a fall of snow." Again he moved north, this time into Sutherland, where he climbed Ben Klibreck (3,154 feet): "Having reached the summit, I saw a large flock of deer skipping along the brow of a hill below, but my view of these beautiful animals was soon intercepted by a cloud of intervening fog."

Four years later Robertson was off once more on his researches, returning this time with an even more impressive 'bag' of summits — Mayar from Glen Clova, Lochnagar, Ben Avon, Cairn Gorm, Sgoran Dubh and Ben Nevis. In Perthshire he was out on one of the Killin hills and also on the high rolling tops above Glen Lyon, between Meggernie and Rannoch. On a remarkable June crossing of the Monadh Liath from Pitmain, near Kingussie, to the headwaters of the Findhorn, he was caught in a thunderstorm of unprecedented violence, being bombarded by hailstones three-quarters of an inch thick and having to steer a part of the way by map and compass. He must have been profoundly thankful to reach a cottage in Strath Dearn, soaked to the skin and dead tired, at 10 o'clock at night. Yet for all this, there is not the slightest trace of boastfulness in his diary records; he is before all else the ardent plant-hunter, and hill-walking is no more than a means — if a pleasant one — to an end. One delightfully 'human' touch not to be missed occurs in the account of his day on Ben Avon. On the descent he had to ford the River Avon, which is noted for the unusual clarity of its water, and he did precisely what so many others would have done in his boots: "Deceived by the apparent nearness of the bottom, which shone so clearly thro' the pellucid stream, I expected the water would reach my knee only; but to my astonishment I plunged at once above my middle."

In any consideration of early tourism in Scotland one comes back inevitably, over and over again, to that indefatigable Welshman, Thomas Pennant. His *Tour in Scotland*, in 1769, and still more his second tour and *Voyage to the Hebrides* three years later make altogether fascinating reading, revealing a traveller of a most lively turn of mind, remarkably far in advance of his time.

"It is but of late," Pennant wrote, "that the North Britons became sensible of the beauties of their country." He discovered many. From the Borders to Sutherland, and out to the Western Isles from Ailsa Craig to Skye, he notes and inquires and describes with tireless enthusiasm. As far as one can tell from his narrative, he never quite reached 3,000 feet; his highest summit seems to have been Beinn an Oir (2,571 feet), in Jura. But how he enjoyed it!

> Gain the top, and find our fatigues fully recompenced by the grandeur of the prospect from this sublime spot: Jura itself afforded a stupendous scene of rock, varied with little lakes innumerable . . . To the South appeared Ilay, extended like a map beneath us; and beyond that, the North of Ireland; to the East, Gigha and Cara, Cantyre and Arran, and the Firth of Clyde, bounded by Airshire; an amazing tract of mountains to the N.E. as far as Ben-lomond . . . Seated on the pinnacle, the depth below was tremendous on every side.

Pennant also climbed the 332 feet of Dun I, Iona's highest hill, and Beinn na Caillich (2,403 feet), the fine viewpoint overlooking Broadford Bay in Skye. But he was no 'tiger' really — the path to the old castle tower half way up the rocky flank of Ailsa Craig he found distinctly alarming — and one is inclined to reach for a pinch of salt when swallowing his remark, "Ascend a very high mountain" on the border of Sutherland and Wester Ross. It is intriguing all the same to speculate on which hill this was — possibly Cul Mor or Cul Beag — just as one wonders who it was who had built the "several lofty cairns" which Pennant found at the summit of Beinn an Oir or, later in his tour, that "of enormous magnitude" on Beinn na Caillich.

In 1773, the year after Pennant had tried his hand at island-going, Johnson and Boswell carried out their no less intrepid Journey to the Western Isles. Unlike their predecessor they did not scale Dun I when they were on Iona, but on one of the three days which they spent on Raasay, Boswell got away to an Alpine start and enjoyed a twenty-four mile exploratory hike which included a Highland dance at the top of Dun Caan, the queer little sawn-off mountain capped by a grassy meadow which is no doubt an ideal place for a reel. This seems to have become quite a fashionable ploy in the early days, for in the *Diary* of a certain Colonel Hawker, written in the year 1813, it is noted of Ben Lomond that "ladies very commonly go up, and sometimes take with them a piper and other apparatus for dancing." What a pity times have changed!

One rather unusual curiosity of the early days associated with Ben Lomond was the window pane of the parlour at Tarbet inn. On this was scratched a piece of doggerel commenting — with some feeling — on the ascent of the Ben, just across the loch. The piece ran to no less than thirty-six lines, so that the "poet", one Thomas Russell, must obviously have been a gentleman of some leisure and much patience. On his own ascent he seems to have set far too hot a pace, for he counsels those who might decide to follow his example to take it more easily, pausing often to taste the "cordial drop" and being sure to have a really long rest at the top. The composition, dated 3rd October 1771, was clearly considered a tourist attraction rather than mere vandalism, for a later visitor to Tarbet, Thomas Newte, passing that way in 1785, says the lines deserve "a less perishable station", and even forty years on, in 1825, the window is mentioned in *The*

Scottish Tourist as being the first object of interest to be noted on entering the inn.

The steep north side of Ben Lomond, obviously a surprise to the majority of those following the ordinary, gentle path from Rowardennan, was meat and drink to writers on the look-out for some sensationalism to liven up their descriptions. Thus John Stoddart in his *Remarks on Local Scenery and Manners in Scotland during the years 1799-1800* finds the face a "stupendous precipice of 2,000 feet" exciting "a degree of surprise arising almost to terror." And Thomas Richardson in his *Guide to Loch Lomond* published in 1799 waxes still more eloquent:

> Ben Lomond rises 3,262 feet above the level of the sea, and on one side is almost perpendicular. We can imagine, perhaps, very few situations, in which the mind is struck with more awful, but sublime sensations, than in looking down from this tremendous eminence on the waters of the lake that undulate below. The fancy, overpowered with a thousand images of danger and of death, recoils with precipitation from the awful prospect; the shivering nerves lose their energy, and the feet cling hard to the surface that supports them, but that seems to tremble under their steps.

Perhaps, however, the prize should go to the diarist Colonel Hawker mentioned earlier. A winter ascent in November 1812 seems to have been fraught with a certain amount of peril:

> To get to the most elevated point of the shoulder we found impossible, as the last fifty yards was a solid sheet of ice, and indeed for more than the last half mile we travelled in perfect misery and imminent danger. We were literally obliged to take knives and to cut footsteps in the frozen snow, and of course obliged to crawl all the way on our hands, knees and toes, all of which were benumbed with cold; and were repeatedly in danger of slipping in places where one false step would have been certain destruction. The going up, however, was comparatively nothing to the coming down, in which our posteriors and heels relieved the duty performed by our toes and knees. . . . We had some very providential escapes, and on our getting below the frozen atmosphere, and again in safety, my guide told us that 'had we slipped nothing could have stopped us.'

In the early days it seems to have been the thing to do to produce a good sound excuse for climbing hills other than mere enjoyment. After he had been out to Staffa on his celebrated visit in 1784, twelve years after the island had been 'discovered' by Sir Joseph Banks, the French geologist Barthelemy Faujas de Saint Fond decided to climb Ben More,

Mull. The expedition was primarily in the cause of science and Saint Fond set out duly equipped with his geological hammers. Yet he was looked at askance by the local youth who had volunteered his services as guide: the latter had produced fowling-pieces and could not imagine why anyone should want to climb Ben More without bringing back a blackcock or two for the pot. Whatever its main purpose, the actual ascent evidently taxed the party to the limit: Saint Fond managed to reach "a great height", but not the summit itself — "In my journeys among the High Alps I never found so much difficulty as here" — and it was left to his American friend William Thornton to save the day by finishing the climb. It is not recorded how many blackcock were bagged.

When exactly Ben Nevis was first climbed is not known. The botanist James Robertson made the ascent in 1771, but so cursory is the mention in his diary that it may well have been almost commonplace even as early as that. Certainly it was by 1787, when a tourist ascent was made by the Rev. James Bailey, vicar of Otley, in Yorkshire, for he and his party found more than thirty small cairns — some with initials and dates left in bottles — near the summit. The diary of Bailey's Scottish tour is in the National Library of Scotland, and if one cares to persevere with his small cramped copperplate, there is an immense amount of interest in it. His description of the Ben Nevis expedition runs to eighteen pages — and it really was an expedition: it consisted of Bailey himself and a Mr Kayne, along with Lieutenant Walker, then stationed at Fort William, who proposed the climb and offered himself as leader, three Highland guides, and a detachment of soldiers from the Fort "to carry our liquors and provisions" — two sergeants and three privates of the Royal Fusiliers — a total of eleven.

Starting at 6 a.m. by way of Glen Nevis, the party had to use hands and knees even before they had reached the halfway lochan. Thereafter the difficulties increased and they found themselves committed to climbing a succession of rock-shelves necessitating combined tactics and up which the last two were hauled by means of a rope and grapnel. The shelves eventually "became a sort of broken and irregular staircase, by which we rose to an ascent far more gentle, but yet so steep that we were obliged perpetually to make use of our hands to assist us." Not far from the summit one of the soldiers fell down insensible and apparently lifeless, but it was found that he had only been making rather too free with the rum. At the top, which they reached in seven hours from Fort William and where they decided they had difficulty in breathing, they spent some time trundling boulders over the edge of the northern cliffs. They then turned to the descent, which was rapid, "although excessively fatiguing, for we were, for the most part, obliged to slide upon our haunches." Finally the party reached Fort William in good order, the whole expedition having occupied nearly thirteen hours.

A somewhat unusual excuse for climbing Ben Nevis came the way of one of the Fort William locals not long after Bailey's epic assault. According to that most adventurous visiter to Scotland, the Hon. Mrs Murray Aust, of Kensington,

> The summit, however, of Ben Nevis, I am told, is a bed of white pebbles, some of them beautiful. There are but few who attain so high a station, it being a very laborious journey to climb that mountain to the top. I learnt, in those parts, another instance of the great love a Highland man has for whisky. A lady of fashion, having conquered that ascent, before she quitted it, left on purpose a bottle of whisky on the summit; when she returned to the fort, she laughingly mentioned that circumstance before some Highland men, as a piece of carelessness; one of whom slipped away, and mounted to the pinnacle of 4370 feet, above the level of the fort, to gain the prize of the bottle of whisky, and brought it down in triumph.*

In September 1801 Mrs Murray Aust spent a fortnight at Rothiemurchus and seems to have enjoyed herself hugely. She climbed the rugged little hill of Ord Ban (1,405 feet), classic viewpoint above Loch an Eilein; she rode to Loch Einich and managed to be thrown backwards off her pony into a peat-bog, and she even rode through the Lairig an Laoigh to Braemar — no mean feat. Her most memorable achievement, however, was an ascent of Cairn Gorm. On this she had four male companions who walked all the way while she herself rode almost to the summit. The party enjoyed splendid views out over Loch Morlich and the dark carpet of the Glen More

---

A Companion and Useful Guide to the Beauties of Scotland (London, 1810).

pines; they walked across to the edge of the plateau overlooking Loch Avon, and they made the detour to the Marquis' Well: "Near the pinnacle of Cairngorm is a well of the finest spring water I ever tasted, and it is also the coldest I ever touched." For those days, long before the decadence of chairlifts was ever even thought of, Mrs Murray Aust's achievement was remarkable; no doubt her summing up was well justified: "To ride up Cairngorm is an arduous task, and to walk down it, a very fatiguing one."

The Cairngorms were clearly coming strongly into favour round about the end of the eighteenth century and the beginning of the nineteenth. Colonel T. Thornton, for example, gives a graphic description of an ascent of the Sgoran Dubh ridge from Glen Feshie in his *Sporting Tour*, written in 1804. Looking down on the sudden eagle's eye view of Loch Einich from the summit, he and his companions were certainly impressed:

> It is impossible to describe the astonishment of the whole party, when they perceived themselves on the brink of that frightful precipice, which separated them from the lake below. They remained motionless for a considerable time equally struck with admiration and horror, the mountain above them to the right chequered with drifts of snow and differing but little from it in colour, the immense rocks to the left, separated by large fissures, the safe abode of eagles, and even the precipices around, appeared to them truly majestic. . . . This lake, bordered by soft sandy banks whose fine but partial verdure scattered over with small herds of cattle, grazing and bleating, and a single bothee, the temporary residence of a lonely herdsman, softens in some measure the unpleasant idea of danger which is apt to arise, while the solemn silence interrupted only by the hoarse notes of the ptarmigants, increasing at the approach of strangers, or by the dashing of the never-ceasing cascades soothes the mind with the most agreeable emotion. Our dinner, which was soon dressed, proved an excellent one, the chief dish consisted of two brace and a half of ptarmigants, and a moorcock, a quarter of a pound of butter, some slices of Yorkshire ham and reindeer's tongue with some sweet herbs prepared by the house-keeper at Raits. these with a due proportion of water made each of us a plate of very strong soup which was relished with a keenness of appetite that none but those that have been at Glen Ennoch can experience. We now drank in a bumper of champaign, gentlemen and servants faring alike, success to the sports of the field, and, with the addition of a tumbler of sherbet and a cordial, were enabled to pack up our apparatus and proceed.

It is of interest to note that elsewhere in his *Sporting Tour*

Colonel Thornton refers to the 'Cairngorms' in respect of the massif as a whole, quite apart from Cairn Gorm itself. Probably, therefore, it was about that time that the old name of Monadh Ruadh, or 'red moors' — in contrast to the Monadh Liath, or 'grey moors', on the opposite side of the Spey — came to be superseded and gradually went out of use.

Wider avenues were beginning to open up. For example, the Rev. Dr. George Skene Keith was shortly to be busy with his height measurements of the chief summits of the Cairngorms, calculations which stand remarkably close comparison with the recognised figures today. But in addition Dr Skene Keith is remembered in the annals of Scottish mountaineering for having done one of the earliest recorded rock-climbs. On 17th July 1810 he and his party were trying to follow the River Dee back to its source high on the plateau of Braeriach and in order to do this without even a minor deviation, it was necessary to keep close to the waterfall which spills over the wall of the Garbh Choire from under a final snow-arch. Two of the party took an easier line, but he and a Mr Warren followed the 'purist' route, up a succession of mammoth blocks set at an angle of seventy to eighty degrees. A notable achievement indeed.

Perhaps the most remarkable traveller of all in the early nineteenth century — and undoubtedly one of the most interesting to take a look at today — was Dr John Macculloch, F.R.S. Born in Guernsey in 1773, Macculloch studied medicine at Edinburgh, but gave up practising in order to devote himself to the geological investigation of Scotland. He was appointed mineralogical and geological surveyor to the trigonometrical survey in 1814 and during the course of journeyings between 1811 and 1821 he visited almost every imaginable corner of the Highlands and islands. South of the Clyde, curiously enough, nothing at all seemed to merit his attention; north of it, his appetite was insatiable. He visited an almost incredible number of the islands from Ailsa Craig to Handa and out to the Flannans, St Kilda and even North Rona, and such are the personal touches which he gives to his descriptions that it is quite obvious that the trips were genuine and not being written up at second hand. His book, *The Highlands and Western Isles of Scotland* — addressed rather

patronisingly to Sir Walter Scott — runs to four volumes and
is garrulous and flowery in the extreme. But it is also highly
humorous in places, and from it, with a little patience, is to be
extracted a most rewarding and illuminating story.

Macculoch's boast, "I have ascended almost every principal
mountain in Scotland," is to be accepted with not a little
caution; and yet it is readily forgiven when one takes a quick
look at his record.

Mainland hills:
Ben Nevis,
Cairn Gorm,
Ben Lawers,
Ben Cruachan,
Carn nan Gabhar, main summit of Beinn a'Ghlo,
Schichallion,
An Teallach, near Dundonnell, Wester Ross,
Beinn a' Bheithir,
Ben Lomond ("many a time have I sat on its topmost stone"),
Ben Vorlich, at the head of Loch Lomond,
Ben Chonzie, Perthshire,
The Cobbler, including the summit rock,
Ben Ledi,
Beinn Lair, Loch Maree,
Cul Beag, Wester Ross,
Ben Venue.

Island Hills:
Ben More, Mull,
Goat Fell, Arran,
Beinn an Oir, Jura,
Beinn na Caillich, Skye,
Dun Caan, Raasay,
Ailsa Craig.

A creditable list in any age. And among many more exploits in
addition he crossed Rannoch Moor — "an inconceivable
solitude, a dreary and joyless land of bogs" — walked round
Loch Coruisk, negotiated Corryvreckan in his ship's long-
boat, and plunged on horseback through the peat-bogs and
across the precipitous sides of Loch Ericht in order to examine
Cluny's Cage on Ben Alder. How many Scots today, one
wonders, are fortunate enough to be able to claim a familiarity
with their country nearly as extensive as all that?

It is difficult to decide which of Macculloch's climbs would

be done on horseback and which on foot; probably most of
them would be walks — certainly this would be so if it is
anything to go by that he thought it of sufficient interest to
comment on Ben Lawers: "It has the additional advantage, to
travellers, that the ascent is so easy as to permit riding to the
summit." For the most part he seems to have gone off alone,
although on at least two occasions he hired local lads to act as
guides. For Lawers he persuaded a young shepherd boy, the
son of the excellent innkeeper Peter MacNaughton, to
accompany him and was worried at having forced him to
accept a shilling in payment, in case he would always expect
the same or more on future expeditions and "possibly end by
demanding five." On the occasion of an August ascent of Ben
Nevis, when it snowed on the summit plateau, he was not so
fortunate in his companion.

> I had with me what is commonly called a guide; a lad who had
> volunteered his services, and whose good humour had secured him the
> place which his talents in pilotage would not have commanded. . . .
> When he found himself in a whirlwind of fog and snow, so thick that we
> could scarcely see each other, and without prospect of any thing better,
> he began to cry; lamenting that he should never see his mother again,
> and reproaching himself for having undertaken the office. . . . He would
> even surrender his five shillings, if I would show him the way down the
> hill.

Fortunately Macculloch was able to set a compass course for
the path — and safety.

One rather surprising failure was Suilven. It is difficult to
accept that Macculloch was put off by the formidable face
which it presents to Lochinver, for he knew well enough its
very different appearance when viewed sideways on. Anyhow,
whatever the reason, he seems to have left it severely alone:

> To almost all but the shepherds, Suil Veinn is inaccessible: one of our
> sailors, well used to climbing, reached the summit with difficulty, and
> had much more in descending.

The date was 1820.

Some of the overnight accommodation 'enjoyed' by these
early explorers of the Highlands must have been quite
incredibly rough and ready. Pennant, in Sutherland, had the
ill fortune to encounter "a gigantic and awful landlady; a
spouse fit for Fin-mac-cuil himself," and Johnson and

Boswell, at Glenelg, had to provide a supply of hay for themselves at the inn, which had none, and sleep on it in their greatcoats. Macculloch for his part makes great play of the wretchedness of breakfast at the "vile pot-house" at Taynuilt prior to an assault on Ben Cruachan. Early on in the morning there was bright sunshine, but so miserably slow was the serving of musty bread, paste-like toast, cold herring, tepid tea and "damp and melancholy" sugar, that the clouds were well down before he was finished and the climb, "which you know will occupy nine or ten hours," could be begun.

Like most of his contemporaries Macculloch was mainly concerned with the views: Ben Lawers headed his list, with Ben Lomond a close second and Ben Nevis nowhere. Yet very obviously he enjoyed far more besides, and it is not hard to appreciate his zest in setting about the final rock problem of The Cobbler, or facing the worst of Highland weather — hail and lightning on the Sgurr of Eigg, downpour on Ben Ledi: "I thought that I had known Highland rain in all its forms and mixtures and varieties; but nothing like the rain on Ben Ledi did I ever behold, before or since." One can readily imagine Dr John Macculloch as one of the more fanatical members of a mountaineering club of today.

His achievements in Skye were, however, anything but impressive. He came to the conclusion that the main Cuillin Ridge was quite unassailable: "The upper peaks are mere rocks, and with acclivities so steep and so smooth, as to render all access impossible." On the only hill he did climb, Beinn na Caillich, he managed to get hopelessly stuck, manoeuvring himself into a position on a rock-face from which he could move neither up nor down and spending the longest ten minutes of his life there before he managed to extricate himself. What of note he did do was to sail into Loch Scavaig and walk round Loch Coruisk, then after dark climb alone for some distance up Sgurr na Stri — a feat which certainly prompted him to think no small beer of himself.

Macculloch may have beaten Sir Walter Scott by a year or two as an early visitor to Coruisk. The latter was there in the summer of 1814 during one of the annual cruises of the Commissioners of the Northern Lights, and that he was deeply impressed by his visit is evident enough in the stanzas

of *The Lord of the Isles*. Lockhart in his *Life* tells how on board
the yacht Sir Walter would often be surprised at night by one
or other of his companions, pacing the deck and muttering to
himself: "At Loch Corriskin, in particular, he seemed quite
overwhelmed with his feelings; and we all saw it, and retiring
unnoticed, left him to roam and gaze about by himself, until it
was time to muster the party and be gone."

Scott, of course, set a pattern of romanticism which seems
today to border on the ridiculous. In art, as in literature, his
influence was immense, and it is not surprising that some
contemporary painters were prompted by his verses to turn to
the Cuillin for their inspiration. George Fennell Robson, who
wandered over the Scottish hills dressed as a shepherd, with
Scott's *Lay of the Last Minstrel* in his pocket, concentrated for
the most part on Perthshire; his *Scenery of the Grampians*,
containing forty outlines of mountain landscape, was
published in 1814. But he looked to Skye too, and his
watercolour of Loch Coruisk — beetling cliffs, stylised
Highlanders and all — is quite agreeably recognisable. It is a
moot point, maybe, whether the same can be said of J.M.W.
Turner's more famous *Loch Coriskin*, one of the sketches
commissioned as illustrations for Scott's poetical works.

On the other side of the Ridge from Coruisk some of the
main corries of the Cuillin seem to have been used as summer
grazings for the black island cattle. Coire na Banachdich,
above Glen Brittle, is said to be the 'corrie of the dairymaid'
and old ruins to be seen there — and also in adjacent Coire a'
Ghreadaidh — would almost certainly be those of shielings of
long ago. Sgurr na Banachdich, the peak which overlooks the
former corrie, presents no undue difficulty and there is no
reason at all why it should not have been climbed often
enough in summer days gone by.

But on the whole the Cuillin summits seem to have been
considered fairly hard nuts to crack — even the tough,
energetic surveyor Thomas Colby failed to 'bag' any when he
visited Skye briefly towards the end of July 1819 — and it was
not until the mid-1830s that they began at last to capitulate.

It was a young Fellow of Christ's College, Cambridge, the
Rev. C. Lesingham Smith, who set the pattern. A strong and
enterprising walker familiar with Switzerland, Italy and

Austria, Smith stayed at Sligachan Inn in 1835, enjoying there good fare and kindly hospitality. Having been defeated by a storm from reaching Loch Coruisk by sea, he set out on foot, accompanied by a local forester as guide. It was a happy partnership. Clearly impressed by Smith's prowess as a walker, the forester proposed a different return route — a short-cut over the ridge into Harta Corrie. The suggestion was no trifling one as it was clear that some serious rock-work would be involved, and a council of war was held; then, the decision having been taken, the two set to work. At first all went well, but soon the going became harder.

> We now came to a steeper part, where we were obliged to crawl upon our hands and knees, and I here found my umbrella a sad nuisance; but the forester's two dogs were much worse, for they were constantly in my way. Sometimes we climbed up a cleft in the bare rock, just like a chimney; and sometimes one was obliged to push the other up; and he in return pulled up the first. A single false step would have hurled us to destruction, and there was, moreover, very great danger that the first man would loosen some stone that might sweep down the hindmost. I once pushed down a tremendous rock, the percussion of which against the crag below sent up a strong smell of sulphur; fortunately for the forester he was above me. In the midst of these difficulties we arrived at a spot where the crag rose up so smoothly and perpendicularly that it was vain to attempt ascending it; we were obliged, therefore, to turn back a little and 'angle round,' as he called it. But in the end we surmounted every obstacle, and stepped forth proudly and joyously upon the very topmost crag.*

An easy descent into Harta Corrie followed, after which the climbers rejoined the ordinary path back to Sligachan. It had been a fine achievement, the first real pioneering in Skye.

The year following Lesingham Smith's rock-skirmish was another notable one for Skye: on 7th July Professor J.D. Forbes, of the Chair of Natural Philosophy in Edinburgh, along with the same forester who had accompanied Smith, Duncan Macintyre, made the first ascent of Sgurr nan Gillean. Macintyre maintained that previously he had made repeated unsuccessful attempts to climb the peak and suggested a new line of approach he had in mind — the line destined to become the classic 'tourist route' of today. It was a great day, a memorable milestone in Scottish mountaineering

Excursions through the Highlands and Isles of Scotland (1837).

history. Forbes was later to earn a wide reputation for his scientific explorations of the High Alps, while in Scotland he seems to have enjoyed a bout of step-cutting on Ben Nevis, and back in Skye in 1845 he and Macintyre 'bagged' Bruach na Frithe for the first time. It is, however, for his triumph on Sgurr nan Gillean that he is chiefly remembered — and maybe envied a little also by those who nowadays have not the remotest hope of finding a virgin summit to tackle.

Needless to say, not all of the nineteenth-century writers have the same serious approach to the hills as Forbes the scientist. Some, like Dr Macculloch, are apt to try a little too hard to be funny and become merely boringly verbose; others, such as the author of *The Scottish Tourist* of 1825, are more ingenuously humorous:

> In high spirits we begin to ascend the mountain [Ben Lomond], but vainly endeavour to keep up with our guide; we suppose it is the philabeg which gives him so much the advantage, for he bounds before us with his basket like a roebuck.

Even after the middle of the century long-winded accounts seem to have been still much in favour. Of Goat Fell, for example, we read:

> Even in the sunshine, it has a grim, haggard, and tempestuous aspect; but when it becomes invested with darkness and cloud, its scowl is positively awful.

One visit in particular had obviously been deeply impressed on the writer's memory:

> Strange voices were heard hissing and moaning among the rifted rocks, while misty forms assumed a definiteness of outline in the gloom which was perfectly startling. Even the old familiar faces of our companions seemed weird and unearthly, and we were fain to close our eyes upon them.

Now, however, a repeat ascent is planned:

> The distance from the inn to the top is set down by certain authorities as being six miles, and it is reckoned pretty clever 'speeling' when the summit is reached in two hours after the start. We *could* accomplish the feat in considerably less time than this, but we don't intend to do anything so foolish. We shall take it leisurely; now paddling in some moorland rill, anon dipping our cup into some lonely well, and again enjoying ourselves in a glorious tumble among the heather.
> Grim and more grim as we ascend becomes the aspect of Goatfell. Now we are panting slowly and silently up a wild rocky steep, anon we

are leaping from one firm spot in a marsh to another, and again we are toiling cautiously along the margin of a deep ravine, wherein a foaming streamlet is seen far below dashing fiercely amongst the boulders and immense rocky fragments of the resounding channel. At length, with hearts fluttering like as many grasshoppers, we attain a kind of level plateau, which was once partly used as a mill-dam, and from which, in the shape of a vast hoary cone, the summit of Goatfell rises proudly up.*

It is a relief to read that the final assault went more easily than expected and that the party reached the summit in good order.

Humour of a different kind is to be found in the well-known 'Ballad of Glen Tilt' written by Sir Douglas Maclagan to commemorate the confrontation of the Duke of Atholl and Professor Bayley Balfour, when the latter, returning from a botanical expedition to Ben Macdhui, insisted that the path through the glen was a right of way.

> Balfour he had a mind as weel
>   As ony Duke could hae, man,
> Quo' he, "There's ne'er a kilted chiel
>   Shall drive us back this day, man.
> It's justice and it's public richt,
> We'll pass Glen Tilt afore the nicht,
>   For Dukes shall we
>   Care a'e bawbee?
>   The road's as free
>   To you and me
> As to his Grace himself, man."

It was one of the hills flanking Glen Tilt — Carn a' Chlamain — which was Queen Victoria's first three-thousander in Scotland.

Somehow one tends to think of Queen Victoria as a little old lady more accustomed to the State processions of London than to doing battle with wind and rain on the high plateaux of the Grampians. Yet the fact is that in 1844, when she did Carn a' Chlamain (3,159 feet), she was only twenty-five, and even in her last 'season' she was still only forty-two. Like all her other Scottish hill-climbs the Glen Tilt expedition was carried out in autumn and this time on a September day of hot sunshine and matchless views. Leaving the glen between Marble Lodge and Forest Lodge, with the Queen and Lady

Days at the Coast, by Hugh Macdonald (Glasgow, 1857).

Sir Hugh T. Munro, Bart.

Indispensable nowadays in mountain survey work: a Bell 47 helicopter off duty at Onich

Blaven and Loch Coruisk, Skye

Canning on pony-back and two more ponies "with our luncheon-box" bringing up the rear, the cavalcade proceeded almost to the top of the hill, where Albert and his retinue of keepers went off on a deer-stalk. The Queen, Lady Canning and Lord Glenlyon continued to the actual summit and had a pleasantly long rest, after which their descent — partly because it was so enjoyable and partly because it had to keep clear of the stalk — lasted until long after the moon was up.

Lochnagar (3,786 feet) almost exactly four years later was much less welcoming. Thick mist racing across the upper thousand feet on a gale-force wind made everything "cold, and wet, and cheerless", yet the Queen seems to have enjoyed the outing greatly, as also did Albert, who disappeared at one point to bag a brace of ptarmigan. Then, another two years after that, the Royal scene shifts to the other side of the Dee valley to Beinn a' Bhuird (3,924 feet) in the main massif of the Cairngorms: a long day of eighteen miles of riding and walking. Ben Macdhui, although once again in mist and a piercing wind, and once again finished in moonlight, was probably the highlight of the Queen's hill-walking career: "*Never* shall I forget this day, or the impression this very grand scene made upon me; truly sublime and impressive; such solitude." And finally her last expedition, in October 1861, was another strenuous one — over Carn an Tuirc (3,340 feet) and Cairn na Glasha (3,484 feet), those pleasant heathery tops on the Aberdeenshire side of the Cairnwell pass. Some of the distant views, Her Majesty noted in her *Journal*, gave her "such a longing for further Highland expeditions."

Sadly, it was not to be. Only two months after that long day on the hills she was to be mourning the loss of the Prince Consort.

Other hills on the Scottish mainland were, of course, becoming gradually popular during this period of royal progress, but little really serious climbing was being done anywhere outside of Skye. There, a variation of Forbes's route up Sgurr nan Gillean was done in 1857 by C.S. Inglis and his party, while the same year that magnificent outlier Blaven was climbed by the poet Swinburne and Professor John Nicol, of Glasgow. It is, however, to the famous Sheriff Alexander Nicolson that pride of place must be given, not only for his actual exploits, which were considerable, but for his boundless, effervescent enthusiasm.

A Skyeman, born at Husabost, not far from Dunvegan, Nicolson did not begin to know the Cuillin at all well until he was thirty-eight; then he most certainly made up for lost time. He began auspiciously by pioneering the delightful western ridge of Sgurr nan Gillean, making a "Vermicular" descent from it by the chimney which now bears his name. In the years that followed he came to know the ridges and corries of the Cuillin in all their moods, by day and by night, in sunshine and in storm, with friends and on his own. Then one wild day in 1873, when he was up in coire Lagan, above Glen Brittle, he caught a glimpse of an impressive black spire rising high above into the eddying mist. The day after, in kinder weather, he made its ascent, after a long but worthy approach round the rim of the corrie, finishing by way of the Great Stone Shoot, the rock and scree gully which was to become so familiar to later generations of mountaineers:

> The climb up the other side of the corrie was stiff and warm and some judgment was required to find a way and still more when it came to circumventing the peak. We did it however without much difficulty, one or two places were somewhat trying, requiring a good grip of hands and feet, but on the whole I have seen worse places.

Thus was the highest of the Skye peaks climbed, later to be named Sgurr Alasdair in Alexander Nicolson's honour — or re-named, possibly, as it is said that it had the earlier name of Sgurr Biorach, the 'pointed peak'. As Mr Seton Gordon has aptly observed: "No man could wish for a memorial more lasting or more wonderful than the dark, wind-swept pinnacle of Sgurr Alasdair."*

In addition to his law work Sheriff Nicolson did much writing — clearly with the greatest pleasure when he was dealing with his beloved Skye. He foresaw something of the island's immense popularity in the years to come and infused into his descriptions a real sense of the happiness that he himself had known.

> Jerusalem, Athens and Rome,
> I would see them before I die:

*The Charm of Skye (Cassell, London, 1929).

But I'd rather not see any one of these three
Than be exiled for ever from Skye.

In 1857 the Alpine Club had been formed, and inevitably fresh enthusiasm took members far and wide in search of new worlds to conquer. It was nevertheless some years before they really began to discover the delights of Skye, although once they did, the fashion was not so slow to spread. It must have been tremendous fun in those early pioneering days before the rocks had been polished white by innumerable 'hobnailers', and the accounts of some of the exploits make fascinating reading for the faithful.

One of the most outstanding achievements was the climbing of the Inaccessible Pinnacle by Charles and Lawrence Pilkington on 18th August 1880. The huge obelisk of the Pinnacle, looking from some directions like a crouching pre-historic monster, forms the highest point of Sgurr Dearg and overtops the O.S. point on the latter by twenty feet. The west ridge, forty feet high, is short and steep with one awkward move; the east ridge is three times as long, and easier, but narrow and exposed. It was the latter which was followed for the first, triumphant ascent. As Lawrence Pilkington recalled long afterwards, for the Jubilee Number of the *Scottish Mountaineering Club Journal* in April 1939:

I first visited Skye in 1880 with my brother Charles. We had only one day's climbing there as we were on our way to fish in the Hebrides with an older brother who did not climb. We had an Ordnance Map with us; on it was marked 'The Inaccessible Pinnacle.' We made the first ascent. I shall always remember that as the noisiest climb I ever had. There was a foot or more of loose rock which had been shattered by the lightning and frost of ages. This formed the edge of the pinnacle and had to be thrown down as we climbed up. The noise was appalling; the very rock of the pinnacle itself seemed to vibrate with indignation at our rude onslaught.

After that we went on to the Hebrides to fish, but the weather proved too dry for any but sea-fishing. We stayed at Tarbert for a week, then caught the steamer at Stornoway and went home. Such an opportunity lost! Most maddening!

My next visit to Skye was in 1883 when Horace Walker, Eustace Hulton and I made the third ascent of the pinnacle — but how different! Not a single loose rock on the ridge; thick mist all round; 3,000 feet below, the sea visible through a rift in the cloud; nothing nearer to be seen. The cloud stretched away and away all round us, a silver sea with the tops only of the highest peaks standing out like black, rocky islands.

No sound! I shall never forget the contrast of those two ascents.*

Thus, gradually, the story of rock-climbing in Scotland was beginning to unfold. It was not to be long before further, significant impulse was added by the forming of the first mountaineering clubs.

*S.M.C.J. Vol. 22, No. 127, p. 63.

6
Meteorology on the Ben

In the library of the Meteorological Office in Edinburgh stands a tall, handsome clock. Its workmanlike appearance and its air of unfaltering precision are in no way deceptive, for it was made as long ago as 1756 and is thought to have been used by Captain Cook on his first scientific expedition to the Pacific. More than a century after that it was taken to the summit of Ben Nevis and there for the twenty-year life of the famous observatory it was the scientists' principal timepiece.

But the old clock is not the only reminder of Ben Nevis in the Meteorological Office: there are fading, historic photographs looking down from some of the walls and there are innumerable books of reference on the library shelves; most interesting of all, perhaps, there are the dozens of jotters and tattered, weather-beaten notebooks — unimpressive to look at, dusty to leaf through — which tell in their own remarkable way the fascinating story of Clement Lindley Wragge.

Wragge was born at Stourbridge, Worcestershire, in 1852. Early on he ran away to sea, finding this a golden opportunity to add navigation to the keen interests he had already formed in astronomy and meteorology. Then, after a spell in Australia as a surveyor, he returned home.

In those days high-level meteorological observatories had been established in many countries throughout the world. Britain, unfortunately, lagged sadly behind, our highest station having been set up at Dalnaspidal, in Perthshire, a paltry 1,414 feet above sea-level. However, some of the leading members of the Scottish Meteorological Society had their eye on Ben Nevis as a possible, most valuable site, and in 1879 plans for the erection of a permanent observatory at the summit were actually prepared; nothing, however, could be done for want of the necessary funds. It was then that Clement Wragge met one of the men most deeply involved in the Ben Nevis project, Alexander Buchan, the secretary of the Society.

His imagination obviously fired, Wragge wrote to Buchan offering to ascend the Ben daily during the following summer and to make observations at the summit simultaneously with observations made at Fort William. Not surprisingly, perhaps, his offer was accepted.

Wragge began his Herculean labour — or penance, as it might perhaps he more accurately described — on 1st June, 1881. It was a wretched summer for weather — the worst for at least ten years, one local farmer commented — and almost from the start conditions were thoroughly disagreeable. Even in the first flush of scientific zeal, it must have called for no small amount of resolution to take, with meticulous accuracy, the series of readings during the ascent, at the summit and again during the descent. At base in Fort William Mrs Wragge was nobly making simultaneous recordings.

In those days, of course, the path up the Ben had still not been constructed. The route Wragge followed went to the north of the 2,322-foot shoulder, Meall an t-Suidhe — one observation point early on being ominously named 'The Peat Bog' — then climbed to the lochan which is now normally reached round the other, southern side of the shoulder from Achintee farm in Glen Nevis. As far as the lochan Wragge rode on pony-back, but thereafter it was footslogging all the way: across the Red Burn, where there was another observation point, to the plateau of Carn Dearg — significantly named by Wragge "The Plateau of Storms" — and so to the summit at 4,406 feet.

What an extraordinary man Wragge must have been! "Unorthodox" and "a king among eccentrics" were descriptions of him given by contemporaries, while in later years another remembered him as "a tall, lanky, gawky, red-headed man with big feet always encased in Blucher boots." He was nicknamed "the inclement rag", and one can easily imagine the ill-concealed laughter that often enough must have greeted him, as he and his big Newfoundland dog Renzo returned bedraggled to Fort William after some long outing on the Ben.

But it is certainly not laughter that is prompted by a study of his diaries. Only admiration. His notes, in the neat copybook handwriting of the day, reveal a passion for accuracy which obviously not even the most exacting conditions could impair. And the never-failing interest which he took in every single thing he met with, from the movements of the gulls, or black slugs in his path, to the Alpine plants or the dimensions of some particularly impressive fog-bow, must have made him a man quite incredibly fascinating to know.

In 1881 the daily observations lasted from June 1st until October 14th and for these Wragge had an assistant by the name of William Whyte. The following year, when the work was carried on from June 1st to November 1st, he had two assistants, Angus Rankin and John McDougall. Departure time was 5 a.m., with arrival at the summit scheduled for 9 o'clock and return to base 3 p.m. The intermediate stations seem to have varied slightly, although they always included 'The Peat Moss' or 'Bog', 'The Lake' and 'The Red Burn Crossing', with, of course, time allowed for a series of readings at the actual top of the Ben.

That Wragge's pages and pages of weather lore were of value is not to be doubted; for his first summer's work he was awarded the Scottish Meteorological Society's gold medal, while the building of the summit observatory might never have taken place had it not been for the interest he aroused. Perhaps all his data would be even more valuable if some ultra-enthusiast of today could be persuaded to do again what he did and provide the necessary comparisons.

But of infinitely more value to the non-scientific layman is the human interest, the story of dogged perseverance, of utter dedication, of sheer heroism, which unfolds as one studies the records. Inevitably titbits of comments have been added here and there, marginal "asides" by way of excuse or explanation or mere artistic enthusiasm, and all these build up into a most vivid overall picture.

Even the very first month of his task was far from free of incidents. On June 3rd it had to be admitted quite apologetically that he arrived five minutes late at the summit; two days after that things were a good deal worse:

> Track covered in parts with snow, and with fog could not readily find my way onwards. So it became *impossible* to reach the Ben by 9.0. Pushed onwards slowly, building cairns as I went. Reached Ben Nevis about 10.13.

Even Wragge was human: on 17th June he overslept as the
alarm did not go off at the correct time; he left at 5.20.! On
21st June he was temporarily laid up with a sprained ankle
and forbidden by his doctor to climb, his assistant taking over.
But by 24th June he was back on the job, keeping strictly to
schedule.

On 3rd July he had to walk the entire distance with no help
from his pony as a reporter of the "Inverness Advertiser" was
with him. The latter did not manage the ascent — small
wonder, perhaps, as the wind was blowing force 8 to 9 all day;
Wragge was at the summit by 9 o'clock as usual. A week later
it was a French visitor from Antwerp who, not surprisingly,
was unable to match his pace. The following day the wind
reached force 11.

Every now and again, breaking through the ordinary
routine details, there are quite remarkable glimpses of this
solitary climber matched day after day against the most
inhospitable mountain in Scotland. Sometimes his hands were
so cold when he reached the rude stone, tarpaulin-covered hut
at the summit that it was impossible for him to turn the key
that opened the door of the instrument cage until he had lit a
fire and thawed out his fingers; even then, on occasion, he had
to hold his pencil in his clenched fist. Once on a bitterly raw
and cold morning of late August, with the wind blowing force
11 and pelting sleet, the only way to cross the final plateau
was by crawling on hands and knees; a correspondent of "The
Times" was with him and the subsequent description of the
day ran to three columns. Once there was a particularly trying
morning when he "had to enter observations on summit on
wood." Now and again he found his instruments smashed by
'tourists'. On one occasion only was there the admission of a
late start (6 a.m.) because of "feeling tired".

There were compensations, of course, apart from the
satisfaction of work more than ordinarily well done:
frequently there were rock-plants at various altitudes to be
identified — some   saxifrage,   maybe,   or   thyme   or
ranunculus — and methodically mentioned in the day's
notes; sometimes there was the music of the wind in the
shattered gullies of the north-facing cliffs; above all there were
the cloud formations, which gave endless pleasure and

immense scope for richly coloured, artistic description as they changed or broke to give far-distant views: "Break in gloomy cloud-fog and glimpse of lovely blue loch, with blue peaks of hills to southward, a grand picture".

Possibly, however, the most absorbing entry of all is that describing the great storm of 14th October, 1881, the day on which for the first time Wragge was unable to reach the summit of the Ben. All the portents that morning had indicated that a cyclone was approaching; even the pony had been loath to move, and it was left behind before the lochan was reached on account of the sodden moor and swollen burns. Fortunately Wragge had with him for company and in case of accident an old and trusted guide named Colin Cameron. By the time the two men reached the lochan, the wind, storming in from the north-north-east, was force 8 to 9. By 8.50 a.m. it had increased to force 11 and the blinding snow and sleet were almost suffocating. At 2,200 feet the going became impossible: visibility at times was down to no more than a yard, and "ice lumps like large eggs had formed on our beards." Renzo the dog presented "a hideous yet most pitiable appearance." There was nothing for it but to turn back and so, after taking the inevitable readings, they retreated arm in arm, at times through snowdrifts more than thigh deep, to lower altitudes and safety.

With his undoubted eccentricity, Wragge does not appear to have been a particularly easy man to get on with and it was probably because of this that when, in the summer of 1883, he applied for the post of superintendent of the new summit observatory, his application was turned down. Three months later he tried again, asking this time to be made honorary superintendent, but once more — rather sadly one feels — he was unsuccessful.

Apart from these glimpses there is nothing more of Wragge to be noted on the Scottish scene. His two assistants, William Whyte and Angus Rankin, did carry out a further series of observations in 1883, but on their own; Wragge himself clearly had thoughts of pastures new — and who can blame him? In 1884 he went back to Australia and established a private meteorological observatory in Adelaide. Thereafter he became Government Meteorologist for Queensland, setting up high-level met. stations on Mount Wellington and Mount Kosciusko. He died in Auckland in 1922. A most remarkable man.

Meanwhile, thanks mainly to Wragge's two heroic summers, work on the observatory had gone ahead. An appeal for funds had been made to the public earlier in the year, the total climbing rapidly to £4,000, with individual contributions varying in amount from £200 down to one penny. Queen Victoria gave £50.

Before any building materials could be carried up, a reasonably adequate road had to be constructed — and this at fairly high speed in order to allow all work to be finished before the onset of the winter snows. In due course "a safe bridle-path, 6 feet wide, with gradients nowhere exceeding one in five," was hacked and gouged out of the hillside from Achintee farm to the summit. This track, at an approximate £800, was the heaviest single item of expenditure, so that in due course a toll was levied on everyone using it — one shilling for walkers and three shillings (later five shillings) for those on pony-back. Permits could be obtained either at a bookshop in Fort William, or from the path maintenance-man at the little half-way hut situated a short distance above Lochan Meall an t-Suidhe — a halting-place which must have afforded welcome shelter in foul weather to many a wet and weary pedestrian.

The original observatory building, with outside walls from ten to twelve feet thick at their base, consisted of one main living-room about thirteen feet square, with three small bedrooms opening off it at one end and at the other end store-rooms, coal-cellar etc. Construction was carried out by a Fort William contractor, James McLean, and was completed — apart from a few minor details inside — in time for the official opening on 17th October, 1883. Work on the path had been finished only a month sooner, so that the last weeks and days must have seen feverish activity indeed. In the minute book of the directors of the observatory there is an entry for 6th September to the effect that application had been made to the War Office for two additional tents, also "beds, kettles and the other furniture of tents" for the use of the workmen. The first superintendent (salary £100) was a Mr

R.T. Omond and it is interesting to note that his chief assistant, and later his successor, was Angus Rankin, who had previously helped Clement Wragge. Rankin was to serve on the observatory staff during the whole of its twenty-year lifetime.

The first building was acknowledged to be compact and strong, but it was at once found to be much too small and cramped to permit satisfactory scientific work being done in it. Indeed, during the first winter it was found to be quite impossible to carry out the full programme of observations. According to a subsequent report by the superintendent:

> As no arrangement had been made for keeping the doorway of the observatory clear of snowdrift, during bad weather almost constant digging was required. Before there was more than two or three feet of snow lying on the open hill-top, great drifts had accumulated round the house, rising almost to the roof, and completely hiding the walls. A passage was dug outwards and upwards through this, which, though quite easily kept clear in fine weather, was constantly filled up as soon as the wind rose, bringing with it whirling snowdrift up the sides of the hill over the buildings. This difficulty was partly overcome by constructing an archway of blocks of snow and tarpaulins over the snow steps leading up from the door, but as no door could be placed at the upper end of this archway or tunnel, there was always the danger of drift blowing down into it, and choking it. On several occasions during the night watches the drift came in faster than one man could shovel it out, and there was nothing for it but to bar the door, and wait till morning, when all hands could be employed to re-open communication with the outside world by an hour or two of spade drill; good exercise, no doubt, but a kind of work not usually included in the routine of an observatory. When the snow reached its full winter depth of ten or twelve feet, all attempts to keep this doorway clear in bad weather were hopeless. Even as late as the beginning of May (1884) the continuity of the outside observations was broken from this cause.

Such tribulations were clearly too serious to be long endured and during the following summer extensive additions were made. These comprised a second, larger apartment to serve as office or laboratory; two additional bedrooms; an extra room for visitors, and a tower equipped with self-recording anemometers and also a doorway for use in winter when the low-level door was blocked with snow. The house proper, inside its thick outer "shell" of granite blocks, consisted of double walls of wood, covered with felt, while the flat roof was of lead. Even when almost completely buried in snow, as it often was, the whole building proved admirably dry and warm.

From the outside, the building seems to have given no hint of the warmth and snugness within. Recording his first impressions in *The Ilkley College Times*, in one of a series of articles describing a six months' stay at the observatory, a certain Mr Drysdale writes:

> Anything more cheerless looking could not well be imagined; a low, straggling, flat-roofed, one-storied building, down whose black walls — of unmortared blocks rough-hewn from the boulders which form the summit — the rain-drops trickled incessantly, while the tattered remnants of the original tarpaulin roof covering, flapping in the stiff October breeze, kept up a drear accompaniment.

From the very first, the observatory was almost literally besieged by visitors. During the summer in which the extension work was going on there were some 4,000, nearly half of these in August. Most, of course, arrived in the afternoon, but some were apt to turn up at any hour of the day or night. All were keenly interested to hear about the observatory, although not a few seemed to imagine that it was a hotel as well and waxed highly indignant when they failed to obtain food and a night's lodging. Matters improved considerably when the special visitors' room was completed and brought into use.

As time went on there was certainly no lessening of the tourist stream; indeed, after the opening of the West Highland railway in 1894, the popularity of the Ben seems rather to have increased. In winter, of course, the occasional strangers who made the summit were treated as honoured guests; in summer, the invasion reached the point of being described as "an unmitigated nuisance". Yet every now and again there was the odd or the unusual to bring some light relief: the visit, for example, of the London tramp looking for work, or the detour made by the Ayrshire man who was trundling a wheelbarrow to John o' Groats in order to raise the wind. According to the records, the oldest visitors appear to have been three octogenarians, the youngest a three-month-old baby girl. Now and again the members of the observatory staff were embarrassed by having tips thrust upon them. And there was the memorable occasion when the temporary Irish cook, already exasperated by the non-arrival of some essential stores from Fort William, was pushed beyond endurance by the 'bounce' of a little Cockney. "'Ere I am at last on top of Scotland's little pimple," proclaimed the latter brightly. To which the Irishman retorted, "Shure, sir, and it's mesilf would be wishing to see it on the back of your neck."

Staff at the observatory normally numbered four and, to judge by the few changes in personnel that were made, they must have got on remarkably well together. The maintenance of the path and the conveyance of stores, letters and newspapers were tasks carried out by another man, resident in Fort William. In summer he would make several trips to the summit every week, bringing up two or three pony-loads of provisions and fuel each time. In winter he still made the climb nominally once a week, but inevitably this was highly uncertain, and when snowfalls had been particularly heavy or bitter winds prevailed, he might be kept at lower levels for as long as five or six weeks on end.

Water supplies came from Wragge's Well, fifty feet from the summit, or else quite simply from roof drainage. When, on rare occasions after a week or two of drought, these sources did fail, supplies had to be carried up on pony-back from Buchan's Well, a thousand feet down the mountainside. In winter a few buckets-full of snow could easily be melted, or in an emergency all that was needed was to open a window and bring in a spadeful.

Even when they were completely cut off from the world below, the observers seem to have known how to enjoy themselves. Indoor amusements included whist, wood-carving and music of various kinds — on one occasion they even arranged for a gramophone recital by telephone from Fort William. Outside there was even greater variety: quoits could be played on the flat observatory roof, and when this sport palled, there were such rival attractions as photography or even hurling rocks down the northern cliffs. Skating was possible for a great part of the year "on a small private pond, ten feet square, made out of an old tarpaulin stretched on the roof and flooded with melted snow." On one occasion at least a curling match was arranged down on Lochan Meall an t-Suidhe. Ski-ing in those days was something of a novelty and it is not surprising that it should have resulted in a mishap which might easily have had serious consequences. One February day an observer's ski came adrift and proceeded to disappear over the cliff-edge, ending up on a ledge more than sixty feet down the face. Its owner decided to try to retrieve it and had himself lowered to the ledge on a rope. Unfortunately the rope cut so deeply into the snow-cornice above that it proved impossible to pull the man up again. Only the timely arrival of a party of Scottish Mountaineering Club members saved the day.

Most popular of all, however, seems to have been the tobogganing. As the superintendent himself wrote: "The pleasures of flying down the hill-side on a toboggan are heightened by the knowledge that, if guided wrongly, or allowed to run too far, the course may end in a precipice or some such obstacle." And as the visitor, Mr Drysdale, also commented, obviously with thoughts of some memorably exciting trips:

> The toboggan course begins at the Second Gorge, three minutes from the observatory, proceeds by a moderate descent for 200 yards, then down McLean's Steep for 100 more, across the undulating Big Plateau for 200, over a twenty-foot precipice filled in with snow, and across the Plateau of Storms 200 more, where it ends just before the continuous steep descent of the Ben commences.

Quite a run for the best part of half a mile.

Animal life at the top of the Ben was scarce, although not wholly absent. Tracks of hares and foxes were often seen, and one winter a family of stoats took up residence among the rocks of the summit cairn, their coats changing to white as the season wore on. They were not long in shifting their quarters to the walls of the observatory and once or twice ventured to look in at the windows. One of the stoats was even spotted inside the building and a hue and cry followed, fortunately with the quarry making a final getaway.

Another winter visitor was a snow bunting, which assumed the role of observatory pet. It came regularly to one of the windows for food and was even found to enjoy the company of its own mirror image.

Life at the top was not, however, without its discomforts, or even indeed its dangers. Occasionally winds were experienced gusting to velocities of over 150 miles an hour and it was not unknown for observers, proceeding on hands and knees, to be bruised by flying snow and ice and to have the greatest difficulty in avoiding being blown over the cliffs. Mention of this is made in the course of one early report:

> On the night of 21st February 1885 a terrific southerly gale blew with almost hurricane force, and stopped all outside observing for fifteen hours. It was impossible to stand or even to crawl to windward, while the most carefully shielded lantern was blown out at once. During the height of the gale the air was full of snow drift, intermixed with which were great lumps of hardened snow that had been torn from the ground by the violence of the wind. One of these flying pieces broke the only window that was above the snow and exposed to the gale, and another smashed half-a-dozen louvres in the Stevenson's screen for the thermometers.

Thunderstorms on the other hand were comparatively rare, seeming mostly to pass by at lower altitudes. Sometimes, however, the lightning conductor would be seen to be tipped with St Elmo's fire, and once, on a June afternoon in 1895, the observatory building itself was struck. The consequences of this were bad enough, although they might well have been worse: the cook was pitched on to his back and rendered temporarily unconscious; the telegraphic apparatus was wrecked, and fire which broke out between the kitchen and the office had to be put out quickly with water and snow before it got out of hand.

The snowfall on the Ben seems to have been very much greater in the old days of the observatory than in more recent times. The maximum depths at the snow gauge were 141 inches in 1884 and 142 inches in 1885, the former towards the end of May, the latter early in April. As a manner of interest, it has been noted in September 1933 every trace of snow had disappeared from Ben Nevis for the first time on record; two years later conditions were similar.

Many more of the statistics which were collected during the life of the observatory were equally interesting. The average amount of sunshine, for example, was found to be only two hours a day, due chiefly to the mist-cap which clings so obstinately to the summit. Only in April, May and June was the monthly average rainfall less than ten inches; December 1900 was the wettest month of all with a total of 48.34 inches.

Over and over again, however — both in Clement Wragge's

notes and in the observatory records — it is phenomena
associated with the clouds which claim the keenest attention.
Coronae of the most brilliant reds and blues and yellows; fog-
bows, both solar and lunar, seen against scudding, dissolving
mist; glories, especially in winter sunshine, when the shadow
of a person standing on the cliff-edge is projected far out on
the mist-floor of the glen below; brocken spectres, centred in
coloured rings against a nearer background of cloud — all
these were seen and recorded on many memorable occasions.

That the Ben Nevis observatory was kept up for 20 years is a
credit to our Victorian forebears. Unfortunately it did not pay;
and when anything as far away from London as Ben Nevis
does not pay, it is looked upon with remarkably little favour.
The fact that it was the first mountain top observatory station
in Europe and probably in the world was evidently not
impressive enough. Already as early as 1887 funds seem to
have been hard to come by, and feeling against official
niggardliness was growing bitter. It was, commented *The
Scotsman* in August of that year, "a telling example of the
neglect against which scientific effort in Scotland has to
struggle." But in spite of public protests the threat of closure
came inexorably nearer. Maintenance of the two stations, on
the summit and at Fort William, was incurring an average
yearly expenditure of close on £1,000. In June 1902 the
directors announced that the observatory would have to be
shut down in October. Questions, some of them pungently
scathing, were asked in Parliament and still the day was
postponed. For two years a private individual, Mr J. Mackay
Bernard, of Kippenross, put up £500. But reprieves could not
continue indefinitely. On 1st October 1904, amid a final storm
of indignation, the observatory was officially closed. A week
later, in a heavy snowstorm, the doors were finally locked and
barricaded.

Later on the observatory was in fact brought into use again
as part of the hotel which was opened at the summit of the Ben
and which survived until the end of the First World War. Here
visitors could have lunch for three shillings, or tea, bed and
breakfast for ten shillings, an offer which seems to have
appealed to many, especially those hoping to see the sunrise.
But the hotel was no more than a poor second best. Many a

Followed by many early travellers including
Thomas Pennant and Queen Victoria; the track through Glen Tilt

The Inaccessible Pinnacle, Sgurr Deag, Skye

The Ben Nevis observatory in winter

Looking south from Braeriach across the Garbh Choire
to Cairn Toul and its Green Loch

Four 'giants' of the Scottish Mountaineering Club:
W. W. Naismith, W. Wickham King, Harold Raeburn
and Rev. A. E. Robertson

meteorologist must have felt that what had happened, when other countries had managed to open and to continue mountain top observatories, was a sorry reflection indeed on our way of doing things.

If, however, we no longer have the services of a weather station, permanently manned, at the top of Ben Nevis, it could be that it will not be long before we have an automatic recording machine there, linked by telephone to a station at Fort William level. This would be an installation of immense value; so too would be machines on other hills, notably Cairn Gorm linked to Glenmore Lodge, which is already an official weather reporting station. When the clouds are low and conditions are rapidly turning sour, how invaluable it would be to know the exact wind speed and temperature and the malice of rain or snow up at the summit cairn! All the records apart, it would make a new and highly significant strand in the evolving pattern of safety on our hills.

7

Cairngorm Stones

Quite literally for centuries a curiously intriguing search has been going on in the Scottish hills. Men and women alike all down the years have been attracted to the rocks and screes and stream-beds to look for the crystals that are sometimes to be found there. In the past the search was intensive and purposeful; nowadays it is no more than intermittent. Yet amateurs and commercially minded have fallen equally under the spell and every now and again, almost as if to keep the interest alive, finds have been made that have been remarkable for both size and beauty.

In 1695, when Martin Martin, Gent., was on Arran, he noted in his celebrated *Description of the Western Islands of Scotland* that there were crystals, much to be prized, in the mountains above Brodick Castle; the Duchess of Hamilton, he said, valued them so highly that she had had a necklace made of them, much to the delight of the local inhabitants, who held her in particularly high esteem. Later on, when out on St Kilda, Martin refers to hexagon-shaped crystals found on the underside of the rocks at the Village Bay landing-place, the largest rather less than four inches in length and two in diameter.

Even in the early days, however, notable discoveries were being made in what seems now to be a much more obvious hunting-ground — in the corries and stream-beds of Cairn Gorm. In the *Geographical Collections relating to Scotland* made by Walter Macfarlane midway through the eighteenth century, an interesting reference occurs in an old description of Strathspey:

> Here is the famous Hill called Kairne Gorum, which is four miles high. Here it is said, there are Minerals: for Gold hath been found here. This Hill aboundeth with excellent Crystall.

A cairngorm is, of course, a hexagonal quartz crystal — quartz being one of the main constituents of granite — varying in colour from smoky yellow to dark brown. The crystals are found in the debris of weathered granite, and most recent finds at least have been made on scree slopes where erosion has been continually moving the surface.

The actual name 'cairngorm' must have found its way into popular usage in the course of the eighteenth century; certainly by the time that the *Statistical Account* came to be compiled almost exactly a hundred years after Martin Martin's island going, it seems to have been fairly generally accepted. There are references in the accounts of three separate parishes. For instance, in the description of Kilbride parish in Arran, Goat Fell is singled out:

> Many transparent stones are found on it, naturally formed into pentagons, heptagons and octagons, and all pointed at the top as if done by art. Lapidaries purchase these stones, and apply them to various uses. They are known among the jewellers by the name of *Arran stones, Cairngorms* and *Scotch topazes*; and are often set in gold for rings, and other ornaments. The colour is generally a dark brown; but some are found of a beautiful yellow, which are reckoned very valuable.

At the same time the writer of the description of the parish of Kirkmichael, in Perthshire, mentions that precious stones in a variety of colours are found on many of the Grampian mountains. But, however much they may vary, all are "denominated by the well known name of cairngorm stones, that being the mountain in which they have been found in the greatest abundance". And in the account of the united parishes of Crathie and Braemar reference is made to Lochnagar and its neighbouring hills: "On them are found pellucid stones, of the nature of precious stones, equally transparent, beautiful in their colour." The writer goes on to give some more specific details, then adds the informative comment: "The first of these stones that attracted notice, and were cut by a lapidary, were found on Cairn Gorm, in Strathspey, but connected with the above ridge of mountains, which gave rise, though very improperly, to the general name of cairngorm stones."

In fact, in the early days, the eastern Cairngorms seem to have yielded much larger crystals than Cairn Gorm itself. Ben Avon in particular earned a big reputation. Near its summit, in 1788, a Castleton (Braemar) woman by the name of Effie

Murray came on one of the largest ever found in Scotland. It was described as being "nearly the size of a child's body at the age of four", measuring 20 inches in length and weighing 49 lb.

There appears to have been an extraordinarily wide discrepancy of opinion as to the value of these rock crystals. For example, Effie Murray's stone was said to have been bought by Farquharson of Invercauld for £40; in 1811, according to Souter's *Agriculture of Banffshire*, it was estimated that not less than £2,000 worth were found on the Cairngorms; in his *Scenery of the Grampian Mountains*, published in 1814, the artist-writer George Fennell Robson mentions the fame of Ben Avon and the precious stones "of the beryl and topaz kind" found on the Invercauld estate, some worth £1,000 and others £500 each; yet in the *Edinburgh New Philosophical Journal* of 1830, although Ben Avon is still reckoned the most productive hill, its cairngorms are said to yield the proprietor "only about £150 or £200 a year."

At one time the plateaux of the Cairngorms must have been quite busy with professional searchers. In summer whole families would resort to the high tops, and the deep trenches which they dug there soon earned them the name of 'miners'. In one place in 1810, apparently, no less than twenty-five acres had been trenched to a depth of from five to six feet. That great chronicler of the hills and first editor of the *Cairngorm Club Journal*, Alexander Inkson McConnochie, tells how at the end of the eighteenth century the workmen at Invercauld were in the habit of going to Ben Avon for a week at a time to dig for cairngorms. Lapidaries, he adds, used to come from the South to purchase the stones or to hire labourers to dig for them at the rate of from five shillings to ten shillings per day. One of the workmen, James Abercrombie by name, was fortunate enough to find a stone valued at £40. Apparently, beside the Allt an Eas Mhoir, the 'burn of the big waterfall', which rises high on Ben Avon, there were the ruins of a building which was the temporary residence about eighty years previously — in 1816 or thereabouts — of a party of miners. The mountaineer, says McConnochie, will frequently stumble across traces of mining operations in the Eastern Cairngorms. He relates also how eight of the miners are said to have met their death from a disease contracted through drinking the gravelly water of the mountain burns.*

John Stoddart, the lawyer and writer, telling of his travels in 1799-1800, describes how he spent a few days at Rothiemurchus after being ferried across the Spey. The 'pebbles' found on Cairn Gorm, he remarks, have the finest lustre of any; but he obviously had no knowledge of Effie Murray's outsize discovery, for he says that the largest stone he had ever heard of was in the possession of Lady Grant of Grant and weighed 16 lb. 11 oz.

Some years later, in the bed of the burn which falls from the Lochan Buidhe towards Loch Avon across the vast, lonely plateau between Cairn Gorm and Ben Macdhui, a real monster was found. A description is given by the Rev. W. Forsyth:

> On the Feith Buidhe there is a narrow gully, broken by ledges and falls. On the left side among the shelving rocks, there is a hole or 'pot', about six feet deep, in which the late James Grant, Rivoan, found quite a treasure of cairngorm stones. When Grant discovered the 'pot', it was full of sand and the debris of granite and spar. On clearing this out he obtained great spoil of crystals of all sizes and degrees of purity. Amongst them was one stone of enormous size, upwards of 50 lb in weight, which was afterwards purchased by the Queen for £50. Sometimes, especially after heavy rains, crystals may be picked up on the surface of the ground, but these, though good as specimens, are seldom of any value. The best stones are got by digging and blasting.†

Queen Victoria herself, on her ascent of Beinn a' Bhuird on 6th September 1850, managed to find a number of cairngorms among the rocks of the summit plateau and duly picked these up. From her *Journal* description, however, they were merely "very pretty" and not particularly outstanding.

Cairngorms, of course, have been in demand ornamentally for a great number of years. From about the beginning of the nineteenth century large ones, centrally set, were used to decorate the circular silver brooch fastenings for cloaks and plaids which are thought to have been made originally by a tribe of tinkers. For a while quite a lucrative business was carried on, but it was not long before most of the really

---

The Cairngorm Mountains I — The Eastern Cairngorms by Alexander Inkson McConnochie. *Cairngorm Club Journal*, Vol. 1 (Aberdeen, 1896).
†*In the Shadow of Cairngorm* (Inverness, 1900).

valuable stones were collected and the native industry faded out. In its place the inevitable 'racket' sprang up and thrived. Details of this were as meat and drink to the cynical traveller and geologist Dr John Macculloch.

> The surface of Cairn Gorm is strewed in some places with fragments of the well-known brown crystals, which are generally named from this mountain, from whatever place they may be procured. But they are by no means peculiar to this spot, since they occur on Ben-na-Chie, in Braemer, in St Kilda, in Arran, at Loch Etive, in Morrer, and in many other situations. They are the objects of a petty and poor trade among the country people and the shepherds, and of a much more profitable one among the jewellers of Edinburgh, who sell Brazil crystal under this pretence, at twenty times its value; thus wisely making a profit out of a silly modification of patriotism. Of the brown crystal indeed, which is thus sold, Cairn Gorm or even all Scotland, does not produce the fiftieth part; and of the bright yellow, and only beautiful kind, it never furnished a single specimen. These stones, in fact, are almost all imported from Brazil, of whatever colour they may be, and often ready cut, at a price of a few shillings, which, by elevating them to the dignity of Scottish crystals, become converted into as many pounds. Such is one of the varieties of vanity. Even on the spot, the shepherds demand guineas for what pence will purchase in London: and if they can find purchasers, I know no good reason why they should not.*

Nowadays, with the supply from the Cairngorms virtually exhausted, most of the stones used for Scottish jewellery are amethysts from Brazil which have had their colour altered by heat treatment to the familiar brownish-yellow. It is interesting all the same to note the variety of localities mentioned by Macculloch. These bear comparison with places singled out more recently by the well-known mineralogist, the late Professor Heddle. He listed, for example, the eastern cliffs of Beinn a' Bhuird, the summit rocks of Bennachie, the east side of Goat Fell, the island of North Rona, and, in Sutherland, the northern crags of Ben Loyal and the east face of Quinag.

Also to be found in the hills apart from cairngorm crystals — although very much more sparingly — are pale green beryl and sky-blue topaz. The former occurs in masses of tiny interlocked crystals to quite large sections of about an inch in diameter, although mostly it is not of gem quality. On the other hand, some of the topaz crystals are as beautiful as

The Highlands and Western Isles of Scotland (London, 1824).

they are rare. Most topaz is, in fact, colourless, although of the colours which do occur, the blues are first in abundance. There are apparently two theories as to the origin of the name topaz: most likely it comes from an old Sanskrit word *tapas*, meaning 'fire', but it was suggested by the Roman writer Pliny in the first century A.D. that the name was derived from the Greek word *topazos*, meaning 'to seek', and that it referred to a somewhat illusory island in the Red Sea. Possibly those who fondly imagine that they will have no difficulty in finding topazes among the rocks of the Scottish hills will come eventually to the conclusion that the crystals are as elusive as Pliny's island.

Topaz is usually found in small broken fragments, although not long ago a most successful modern collector described having seen a fully terminated flawless crystal an inch long and almost half an inch in diameter. He commented nevertheless that a searcher nowadays could be considered very lucky indeed if he were to come across any crystals of this kind. Back in 1795 Beinn a' Bhuird and Ben Macdhui were mentioned in the *Statistical Account* as being two hills where topazes were to be found.

What then really are the prospects of success for the searcher of today? "I can say," writes one enthusiast, "that good crystals are still around, but collecting is a very strenuous pursuit after one and a half centuries of exploitation. They nearly always occur between the 3,000 to 4,000-foot level, where the winds are snell, the mist is wet and the distances are vast. It takes as much dedication to stone-hunt in the Cairngorms as it takes to climb their windy crags. Happily for the real enthusiasts, this rules out competition from most lapidaries, who seldom get beyond the well-combed beaches (agate)." And then he adds: "The Arran granite — which is much younger — has smoky quartz of high quality, but unless one is lucky enough to strike a pocket of crystals, it is otherwise sparsely distributed. Surface crystals were no doubt common enough 150 years ago, but by then local shepherds were gathering them for sale to commercial collectors."

It would seem therefore that finds of really good quality cairngorm crystal are now relatively few and far between.

Much of the material that is discovered — usually on scree-slopes — is from the tailings of old workings, and traces of these have mostly vanished long ago due to successive rock-falls and erosion. Unworked pockets are rare and, of course, occur over a wide area, often at considerable distances from the usual hill-routes. In addition, due to the age of the rocks, the crystal often has a coating of oxide which is difficult to remove without spoiling the glaze. All in all, therefore, good specimens are particularly hard to come by.

And yet, as one of the experts adds, there can still be remarkably worth-while rewards. "Large crystals have been found occasionally. I personally have seen about a dozen in the last ten years; most of these weighed from 1 ½ to 2 ½ lbs. The largest I myself have found is not complete, but is just over 3 lbs." Not indeed repetitions of the remarkable good fortune of an Effie Murray or a James Grant, but sufficiently notable perhaps to set others on the hunt with more than adequate optimism.

8

Golden Age

The earliest mountaineering club to appear on the Scottish scene seems to have had its own rather original ideas as to how things should be done. Founded in the year of the Battle of Waterloo, the Highland Mountain Club of Lochgoilhead met only once a year, at midsummer. But what its activities lacked in frequency they evidently made up for in jollity. Festivities lasted for the best part of forty-eight hours, the first night being spent at the top of "a lofty mountain" and the second in a protracted dinner at the local hostelry. Bagpipes and flag-bearers led off the climb itself in splendid style, while the spell on the summit — prudently safeguarded by the provision of a commodious tent — was enlivened by Gaelic conversation and toasts, interspersed with salutes of musketry. One cannot escape the feeling all the same that the viewing of sunset and dawn, ostensibly the *raison d'être* of this annual expedition, must have seemed somewhat tame by comparison with the other events on the programme.

Equally unusual, although in rather different ways, was the better-known Gaiter Club, founded in 1849. According to their motto, *Flumina amo silvasque*, members were meant to hold the countryside in high esteem, the aim of the club being to enjoy beautiful scenery quite informally. Some of the social functions — each of which was dubbed a 'Gaiter' — were in fact outdoor affairs. They were, however, meant to be devoid of all muscular exertion and even after-dinner speeches had to be delivered sitting down, so that the club can hardly be said to have set any great example of achievement on the hills. Some of their remaining members — also known as 'Gaiters' — were, however, closely associated with the Scottish Mountaineering Club in its earliest years, Gaiter (Professor G.G.) Ramsay becoming the first president of the latter club. Certainly the spirit of fellowship which they cherished above all else was one useful characteristic which they brought with them.

Professor Ramsay was also one of the founders of the Cobbler Club, in 1866, an altogether more energetic and enterprising body than the Gaiters. The aim this time was "to climb the Cobbler and whatever other worthy hill could be reached in the course of a Saturday expedition from Glasgow, and to crown the labours of the day by such an evening of social enjoyment as can only be spent by those who have had a sniff of true mountain air during the day. The exploits of the Club ranged from Tinto to Ben Lomond and from Dumyat to Dumgoyne."*

Edinburgh, of course, was not to be outdone by Glasgow, and a small group of hill-walking enthusiasts, named appropriately 'The Tramps', were meanwhile enjoying outings together on a number of the Scottish hills. All of them, along with several of the Cobbler Club, subsequently became members of the Scottish Mountaineering Club.

The door was now opening wide. In Dundee in April 1886 the Dundee Rambling Club came into being with fourteen original members. Two months later their first club walks took them from Clova to Braemar by way of Glen Doll and Glen Callater, thence back the following day through Glen Tilt to Blair Atholl. But they were by no means a 'summer only' club, one early hill-climb being Ben Macdhui in spring, another Ben Vorlich in November, when the condition of the snow was good but the cold intense and visibility poor. As one verse of a poem contest for members put it:

> Our fortune's our ice-axe, our bonnet, our boots;
> Our food is of bannocks, Glenlivet, cheroots;
> Our comforts are many — yes, plenty — hoot-toots!†

It was in the course of a truly summer expedition that the Cairngorm Club was founded. On 22nd June 1887 a party of six made the ascent of Ben Macdhui in order to celebrate Queen Victoria's jubilee with a midnight bonfire and fireworks. The following morning they dropped down to the Shelter Stone prior to making their way over Cairn Gorm to Speyside, and it was while they were resting at Loch Avon level that they decided to form themselves into the club which,

*S.M.C.J. Vol. 23, No. 136, p. 254.
† ibid. p. 257.

from these small beginnings, has grown and flourished now for the best part of a hundred years. The resolution of the six was confirmed in Aberdeen on 9th January 1889 and the first official meet — appropriately with Cairn Gorm as the objective — took place in the following July. Thus, by a matter of days, this was the first strictly mountaineering club to come into being in Scotland.

A letter hidden away on the yellowing files of *The Glasgow Herald* gives the clue to the formation of the Scottish Mountaineering Club. The writer of the letter was W.W. Naismith, his subject a 'Proposal for a Scottish Alpine Club'. The date on which it was written was 10th January 1889 — the day after the official founding of the Cairngorm Club. In the course of his appeal to other hill-lovers Naismith wrote:

> It is almost a disgrace to any Scotsman whose lungs and heart are in proper order if he is not more or less of a mountaineer, seeing that he belongs to one of the most mountainous countries in the world. In the hope of encouraging the pursuit among our countrymen I would suggest the formation of a Scottish Alpine Club, membership in which would involve a certain number of ascents either (1) in the Alps or (2) in Scotland. The qualifications for class I might be fixed at say three peaks of 12,000 feet each and three passes of 10,000 feet, and for class II six mountains of 3500 feet at least. A single trip to Switzerland would suffice for the former, and a few weeks among the Grampians for the latter — Baddeley's guide to the Highlands giving a list of seventeen summits of the requisite height, most of them of easy access.

The highly interesting correspondence which ensued led, a month later, to a meeting of enthusiasts in the Christian Institute in Bothwell Street, Glasgow, and the official birth of the S.M.C.

It is perhaps worth mentioning in the passing that Naismith's recommendation that certain qualifications should be insisted on for membership of the club was duly taken up. It has, however, been varied in that Alpine achievements, while lending weight to any application, have very rightly not been considered sufficient in themselves (except in the early days when Alpine Club members were accepted). Only a thorough knowledge of the Scottish hills, at all seasons and extending over a number of years, with rock and snow-climbing experience included, is the normally accepted standard of entry.

The club seems to have got off to a start which on the face of it was remarkably slow. The first official meet — attended by only seven members, three of whom were professors — did not take place for two years and then it was a comparatively humble affair at the Crook Inn in the Borders, with the highlight a misty ascent of Broad Law (2,754 feet) on the Peebles-Selkirk boundary. To recall that by then no less than eleven years had elapsed since the Pilkington brothers had climbed the Inaccessible Pinnacle in Skye suggests an absence of initiative which is hard to understand.

It would be unjust, however, to accept this as correct. Within a year of the club's formation the first number of the *Journal* — greeted apparently with many misgivings — had made its appearance; to begin with this record of members' activities ran to three numbers annually, No. 6 carrying Munro's historic *Tables*. Also, unofficial meets were immediately popular, and no less than four unsuccessful attempts were made on that deep, dark, disagreeable fissure, the Black Shoot of Beinn Eunaich, before it was finally climbed in May 1892 — one of the first pure rock-climbs to be made on the Scottish mainland. Nor were things altogether quiet in Skye, where Professor J. Norman Collie, Manchester-born Scot, was already fairly embarked on his brilliant mountaineering career; since 1886 he had been busy familiarising himself with the main Skye peaks and soon had some memorable exploits to his credit, invariably with his boon companion, the famous guide John Mackenzie. In 1891, for example, his crossing of the Thearlaich-Dubh gap with Mackenzie and W.W. King solved one of the most interesting 'problems' of the Cuillin Ridge and indicated the shape of things to come in his own climbing adventures.

That last decade of the nineteenth century was without a doubt the Golden Age of Scottish mountaineering. Certainly it is difficult enough for the enthusiast of today to think of it without a good many pangs of envy. The scope for exploration and discovery throughout the length and breadth of the Highlands was unlimited: one after another the great routes on Ben Nevis, in Glencoe and in Skye were falling to determined assaults; dimly at first, but very surely nevertheless, the pioneers were beginning to realise the enjoyment that is to be found in winter mountaineering in Scotland. In the English Lake District, where rock-climbing had got off to a slightly earlier start than in Scotland, the 'gully and chimney period' was gradually giving way to the more advanced 'ridge and arête period'; in the Alps, too, it was a time of advance, witnessing as it did the rise of guideless climbing, chiefly owing to the inspiration of the great A.F. Mummery. The earliest of the pioneers in Scotland were almost without exception Alpine-trained men, so that inevitably achievements on the home hills were made to stand comparison with what was being done abroad. Indeed for long enough the snow and ice climbing of Scotland was looked on essentially as training for better things elsewhere; it was to be many years before it gained the recognition it deserved — acceptance as a supremely satisfying variety of mountaineering in its own right.

Of the many interesting personalities of those early club days perhaps W.W. Naismith, the 'father' of the Scottish Mountaineering Club was the most outstanding. Yet curiously enough he himself was modest and retiring almost to a fault. For instance, at the meeting called to discuss the formation of the S.M.C. he sat at the back of the hall and took no part in the proceedings; persistently, despite all the later efforts at persuasion by his fellow-members, he refused to accept office as president of the club. On the other hand he is still affectionately remembered as a man of strong Christian character, one of his convictions being, for all his love of the hills, an avoidance of Sunday climbing. Naismith had climbed Ben Lomond before he was fourteen and was already acquiring Alpine experience in his twenties. (It is interesting to note that a solo winter's day at that time on Ben More in Perthshire made him realise that the higher Scottish hills under snow needed to be treated every bit as seriously as Alpine peaks). It was not, however, until he was nearly forty that his most memorable achievements were accomplished and even then they were almost all crowded into the six seasons 1893 to 1898. Yet these years were truly remarkable. Even a quick glance through the climbing guide-books is enough to give a fair idea of his prowess. The Arrochar hills and Arran, Ben Nevis and Skye, each of these novel 'playgrounds' allowed his initiative almost unlimited scope, and it is quite extraordinary how many of his discoveries became 'classics'. One thinks, for example, of the traverse of The Cobbler, over the Centre Peak and up Right-Angled Gully — later to be scratched so smooth by countless bootnails; of the Spearhead Arête on Beinn Narnain; of the now familiar 'trade route' outflanking on its east side the Great Tower on Ben Nevis's Tower Ridge; of his time-honoured masterpiece of ledge and crack up the exposed face of the Bhasteir Tooth in Skye. He could even have claimed the first ascent of what was probably the last unclimbed peak of the Cuillin, the north top of Sgurr Coire an Lochain. And in addition to all this, a still more familiar memorial of him has for long been his 'formula', the well-known and remarkably accurate method of calculating the time needed for a day on the hill — an hour for every three miles, plus half an hour for every thousand feet of ascent. Scottish mountaineering was fortunate indeed to have a man of Naismith's calibre to set the standard from the very first days.

Professor Norman Collie's mountain travels took him to many more distant corners of the world than were ever known to Naismith. The Alps, the Lofoten Islands, the Canadian Rockies, the Himalaya — he was with Mummery on the latter's ill-fated expedition to Nanga Parbat — all received his keen attention; everywhere his achievements were outstanding. Yet it was the hills of Scotland, and above all of Skye, which claimed his deepest affection. Passing mention has already been made of his great companion, the local guide John Mackenzie. John climbed among the Cuillin for over fifty years and with Collie pioneered many of the routes which have been household words to four generations of rock enthusiasts — especially notable perhaps the ledge which curls round the crown of Sgurr Mhic Coinnich, 'Mackenzie's peak', and of course the Cioch, the striking knife-edged tower out-thrust from the wall of Sron na Ciche, the mecca of countless thousands of the faithful.

A dozen years before he first climbed the Cioch, Collie had made a remarkable onslaught on the crags of Glencoe and Ben Nevis. In 1894, following the S.M.C.'s Easter meet at Inveroran, he mounted a most determined rock-climbing campaign, with Godfrey Solly and Joseph Collier as his equally experienced rope-companions. Camping under the immense cathedral-face of Buachaille Etive Mor, then virtually unexplored, this powerful trio pioneered the first-ever route — Collie's Climb — up 1,000 feet of rock and ragged heather at the south-east corner of the crags. Thereafter they moved on down to the western end of Glencoe and carried out some notable exploration in the then unknown fastnesses of Bidean nam Bian. Best of all, an interlude on Ben Nevis before returning once again to Bidean provided them with the first complete ascent of the Tower Ridge, "a superb climb of about 2,000 feet of ice, snow and rock that took about five hours of continuous work" — the finest climb Collie had ever made in Scotland.

It was in 1891 that Professor Collie had his celebrated encounter with Am Fear Liath Mor, the Big Grey Man of Ben Macdhui. He is not the only one to have known unreasoned yet intense terror on that bare, windswept plateau, yet his is the story most often related:

> I was returning from the cairn on the summit in a mist when I began to think I heard something else than merely the noise of my own footsteps. For every few steps I took I heard a crunch, and then another crunch as if someone was walking after me but taking steps three or four times the length of my own.
>
> I said to myself, 'This is all nonsense'. I listened and heard it again but could see nothing in the mist. As I walked on and the eerie crunch, crunch, sounded behind me I was seized with terror and took to my heels, staggering blindly among the boulders for four or five miles nearly down to Rothiemurchus Forest.
>
> Whatever you make of it I do not know, but there is something very queer about the top of Ben Macdhui and I will not go back there again by myself I know.*

A strange story indeed, not really provocative of laughter. For Collie was a distinguished scientist, a Fellow of the Royal Society, a man of reticence, austere and rather withdrawn, a man not given to suffering fools gladly. If in fact it was his imagination which played him a trick, it is odd in the extreme that of all the mountains he was familiar with across the face of the earth, Ben Macdhui should have been the one where this occurred; Ben Macdhui, where so many other walkers

*Cairngorm Club Journal, Vol. XI, No. 64, July 1926.

and climbers over the years have had experiences, comparably eerie, of the spine-chilling spectral Grey Man.

Some of the earliest meets of the Scottish Mountaineering Club must have been truly memorable events — times of discovery and shared experience and jovial fellowship never quite matched in later years. Numbers to begin with seem to have been quite small, no more than a handful by the hotel fire of an evening, recapturing all the most exhilarating moments of the day just past. Theirs no doubt was the mood caught so admirably by the founder and first editor of the *Journal*, J.G. Stott, when he ended the club song he had composed:

> From the sunrise flush, when the hill-tops blush,
> Till the moonbeams quiver on the ice-bound river,
> We push attack and foray, over ridge and peak and corrie,
>   When we go up to the mountains in the snow.
> When the long day's done, and the vict'ry's won,
> And the genial whisky toddy cheers the spirit, warms the body,
> Then the ptarmigan and the raven, far aloft above our haven,
>   Hear our chorus faintly wafted o'er the snow.
>   *Chorus.*
> Oh, my big hobnailers! Oh, my big hobnailers!
> How they speak of the mountain peak,
> Of lengthy stride o'er moorland wide,
> Oh, my big hobnailers! Oh, my big hobnailers!
> Mem'ries raise of happy days
> Upon the mountain side.

The opening of the West Highland Railway in August 1894 changed the whole pattern of travel to the west and north, and it is hardly surprising that Easter meets were promptly arranged for Fort William in both 1895 and 1896. To many of those who attended, the attractions of Ben Nevis came as a complete revelation, and although heavy snow conditions in 1895 put the Tower Ridge out of court, no less than three parties did Castle Ridge and one the remote 1,500-foot North-East Ridge of Ben Nevis's near neighbour, Aonach Beag. The following year eight Alpine Club members attended and although their performance was not particularly distinguished, the meet as a whole produced an impressive total of new routes.

Highly typical of the enthusiasm — almost the exuberance — of those early days were the exploits of William Tough and William Brown. Forming what was obviously a

Stalwarts of the past; centre Sir Hugh Munro. At the
Scottish Mountaineering Club's meet at Dundonnell in 1910

Buachaille Etive Mor

most congenial rope-partnership, these two are best remembered for their early exploration of the great north-east corrie of Lochnagar, choosing what has since then been known as the Tough-Brown Ridge — as the guide-book puts it, "this massive structure of dizzy, holdless slabs." It was, however, three months earlier than this, at the end of May 1895, that they carried out their most remarkable *tour de force*, an assault on the North-East Buttress of Ben Nevis.

> It was the last Easter Meet that brought this ridge into fame. From being an unnamed and unhonoured incident upon the cliff-face, it became an object of ambition to a large circle of climbers, the chief topic of the smoke-room at nights, and the focus of many critical glances during the day. It would also have been climbed had the ice upon the rocks not forbade the attempt; but though spared at Easter, it stood marked in the intentions of several parties, of which Tough and I formed one.

Leaving Edinburgh on the night train to Inverness, they reached Kingussie at 3.50 a.m. on Saturday. It was raining and dense mist hung low on the sodden hillsides. "Very grey and miserable," commented Brown in his subsequent description.* Pushing on from Kingussie on their bicycles, they were just crossing the watershed of Scotland when a loud report proclaimed a puncture. There was nothing for it but to wheel three miles to Laggan Hotel, but as no help was forthcoming there, they continued the further thirteen miles to Tulloch station, on the West Highland Railway, Tough "mounting the remaining bicycle, with a pyramid of ropes, axes, and rucksacks piled up on his shoulders, while his fellow-traveller half-walked, half-trotted alongside." Lunching in Fort William, they set off again at 1.12 p.m. and after a wearisome slog up and over the lower, grassy slopes of the Ben, reached the Allt a'Mhuilinn glen and eventually, at 5.30 p.m., the foot of the buttress. Thunder had been grumbling round the Lochaber hills all afternoon, and it was so wet that they even discussed retreat. "Not even in Skye have I seen rocks so wet. There was quite a respectable waterfall coming off the ridge, and innumerable smaller ones that in England would draw hosts of worshippers." Then, unexpectedly, they were reprieved: the rain eased and the mist

*S.M.C.J. Vol. 3, No. 18, pp. 323-31.

lifted, so that they were able to carry on with the climb. All went well and — despite wet and weariness — with obvious enjoyment, especially as they got higher, above the second platform.

> There are little towers up which the leader had to scramble with such gentle impetus as could be derived from the pressure of his hobnails upon his companion's head. There are ledges (not very terrible) where it is convenient to simulate the grace of the caterpillar. A sloping slab we found too, where the union of porphyry and Harris tweed interposed the most slender obstacle to an airy slide into the valley.

At 10.5 p.m., with a shout of triumph "which was taken by our friends the meteorologists that some very noisy trippers were approaching," they reached the summit and the observatory. After some welcome coffee and an hour's sleep snatched between midnight and 1 a.m., they descended the path to Fort William and caught the 4 a.m. mail-gig back to Kingussie. By 6.15 in the evening they were safely back in Edinburgh, "after forty-five hours of continuous travelling."

And then, after all that, it turned out that theirs was not a first ascent. Shortly after their exploit it came out that the North-East Buttress had in fact been climbed for the first time three years previously by the three Hopkinson brothers.

Another 'giant' of the earliest days of the S.M.C. was William Wickham King, who died in 1959 at the age of ninety-seven and who had been a member of the club for sixty-eight years. A solicitor from Stourbridge, Worcestershire, King had immensely wide mountaineering experience in many districts of the Alps, as well as in Norway, the Pyrenees and Tyrol. It was, however, in his explorations of the Cuillin — and in particular of the chimneys there — that he seemed to come most completely into his own. Brief mention has been made earlier in this chapter of how in 1891, along with Professor Norman Collie and John Mackenzie, he crossed the celebrated Thearlaich-Dubh gap. He had in fact been to Skye for two climbing holidays prior to that, and during the years following, both in Scotland and in the Alps, he came to know well most of the illustrious mountaineers of the day. In August 1898, with G. Bennett Gibbs and John Mackenzie, he managed to force a route — largely subterranean — through the huge cave-gully between Am

Basteir and its lower but no less formidable subsidiary, the Bhasteir Tooth. Exploration of the route occupied no less than four days, and a great deal of time had to be spent in moving obstructions and threading an intricate passage behind successive chockstones. At one point a small hole led into a vertical funnel 40 feet high, which had to be climbed in almost total darkness. On a later occasion an august president of the S.M.C. became stuck in the chimney and the advice given in the early guide-book, "Nobody measuring more than 38 inches in girth should try this route," was doubtless very sound indeed. Unfortunately it has been reported that in 1924 the final chimney was completely blocked by a fall of rock.

It is a pity that the meet of April 1897 was nothing like so successful from the mountaineering point of view as those of the two preceding Easters at Fort William had been. A novel idea had commended itself to the club committee — to charter a steam yacht and use this as a luxurious base from which to attack the Cuillin Ridge. In due course the *S.S. Erne* set sail from Oban, rounded Ardnamurchan Point and dropped anchor in Loch Scavaig. All might have been triumphantly well — had it not been for the weather. Stormy seas whipped to fury by a south-westerly gale had made the sail-in anything but pleasant and the anchorage none too secure. The *Erne*, therefore, was headed back to Loch Scresort under the hills of Rum, where several of the party climbed Allival and Askival, and thence back to the mainland for exploration of the peaks above Loch Nevis and Loch Hourn. Two obvious choices there were Ladhar Bheinn and Sgurr na Ciche. The former provided a somewhat moist battle in a gully defended by new snow on inhospitable, mossy ledges; the latter relied for its defiance on its long distance from base at Inverie, and the two who visited its shapely top had a gruelling race against the clock to return to the yacht by sailing-time at 6 p.m. The last picture we have of the meet is of the evening sail back to Oban, members and guests dancing reels on the deck of the *Erne* against the gold of an island sunset.

Unfortunately the experiment was never repeated; the weather had played spoilsport all too successfully. Indeed it is remarkable how seldom since then, even on a small scale, mountaineering and sailing on the West Coast have been brought together in what surely on occasion at least must be an ideal combination.

Two of those on board the *Erne* for that week-end in 1897 were soon to be playing leading parts in the story of Scottish mountaineering — Harold Raeburn, then an S.M.C. member of four months' standing, and one of the guests, W.N. Ling. For the latter this was the first of a record 105 attendances at meets of the club. With Raeburn — quite apart from his achievements on the home hills — he was to be associated in a whole series of brilliant guideless climbs in Norway, the Alps and the Caucasus.

Every now and again in mountaineering, as of course in every other outdoor pursuit, stars shine out more brightly, more noticeably by far than any of their rivals. Such a star was Raeburn. Admittedly the opportunities were there for the seizing; but in fact he did immeasurably more than just collect the easy pickings. With an unerring eye for a worth-while route, he originated a whole string of 'classics' all over Scotland, from Arran to Sutherland and from Skye to Lochnagar, leaving an imprint of greatness which the years have done nothing to lessen. Glencoe and Ben Nevis were probably his happiest hunting-grounds. Routes like the Church Door Buttress on Bidean nam Bian and, on Buachaille Etive Mor, Crowberry Gully — of which he made the first three ascents — speak for themselves; on Nevis, among a number of 'firsts', his solo successes on Observatory Buttress and Observatory Ridge command very special admiration.

Two decades later Raeburn's skill was undiminished. In 1920 he was on Kangchenjunga and reached 21,000 feet. The following year he went out to Everest with the first reconnaissance expedition as leader of the climbing team of four. Unhappily his health broke down and he had to be evacuated to hospital. Two months later, after a most arduous journey, he rejoined the expedition. But it was not to be. He was destined never to regain his old vigour; a complete breakdown supervened and after four years of increasing weakness he died. In the obituary notice of his old friend and rope-companion, W.N. Ling wrote: "His own native hills were the first to receive his attention, and he quickly showed that he possessed in a marked degree the qualifications of a mountaineer. Light, wiry and active, with supple limbs and a beautiful balance, he added to his physical gifts an indomitable will, a sound judgment as to routes and possibilities, and a fearless self-reliance."* It was tragic indeed that despite all his brilliance he was denied the realisation of his supreme life's ambition — getting closely to grips with Everest.

Although only eight years younger than Raeburn, Ling himself lived to the age of eighty and thus seems to have belonged to a much more recent generation. It is, however, mainly for the exploratory work he carried out in the far north-west in the early years of this century that he is remembered in Scottish mountaineering history.

Back in 1892 a significant rock-climb had been done — appropriately enough up the formidable face of Suilven's Grey Castle, one of the toughest-looking bastions in Sutherland — by two well-known members of the Alpine Club, Charles Pilkington and Horace Walker. And three years later the climb had been repeated — by Professor Ramsay and his son Malcolm (all ignorant, as it happened, of how they had been beaten to it). With these exceptions, however, the wilds of Sutherland and Wester Ross remained largely unexplored — not surprisingly when one thinks of the rigours of travel long before the days of modern roads and the modern motor car. Even as late as 1909, Ling was able to give a dramatic description of an approach to Beinn Lair and Beinn Airidh Charr:

> It is a far cry to Poolewe, where we established our headquarters, thirty-six miles from Achnasheen Station, if one goes by land, which one is obliged to do, unless the weekly boat happens to synchronise with the time at one's disposal, but there is a mail coach which gets there after a somewhat lengthy journey, and a motor car can be hired from the hotel at Achnasheen.
>
> We chose the latter course, but got rather a shock when we were invited to get into a motor *char-à-banc*, constructed to carry fifteen tourists. Our modest weight was insufficient to keep the vehicle from bouncing into the loch, so we were obliged to carry some ballast in the shape of bags of corn.

*S.M.C.J. Vol. 18, No. 103, p. 26.

The steering wheel was geared very low, and we exchanged glances of amused apprehension, when our chauffeur spun his wheel at the first corner, but he proved capable of conveying us to our journey's end in three hours without catastrophe.*

It is quite remarkable how almost every hill of importance in the north-west, almost every notable rock-face, was first explored by Ling, nearly always in association with his great friend George Glover. What wonderful times they must have had! The first to climb out of Toll an Lochain, spectacular eastern corrie of An Teallach; the first to attempt a route on the magnificent gneiss cliffs of Beinn Lair; first on Martha's Peak of Beinn Airidh Charr; first on Beinn a' Chaisgein Mor; first on Sail Mhor of Beinn Eighe; on Ben Hope, on Foinaven, on Beinn Deag Mhor — the list seems quite monotonous. One can readily imagine the sense of expectancy with which they would set off, invariably in late spring or early summer, in some veteran car of dubious performance to try for further discoveries of their rather specialised variety of climbing — steep and airy and above all new — in some of the finest mountain scenery in Britain.

As the new achievements began to proliferate, so too did the books about them. And what grand reading many of them still make today! There is an exuberance, almost a naïvety about some of the descriptions which could not possibly be recaptured now. The freshness has worn off, of course. The straightforward account of a climb which has been done a thousand times and more would seem to be quite worthless; certainly it would be hopelessly 'dated' alongside much of the terse, irreverent realism that tries so hard nowadays to have the reader gripping the arms of his chair. Yet it is a pleasure to get back, now and again at least, to occasional unashamed wholesomeness, to enjoy unvarnished narratives written before there were any heroes to de-bunk or any rivals to out-boast.

One such book, *The Highlands with Rope and Rucksack* by Ernest A. Baker, although published in 1923,† tells the story of several classic exploits just after the turn of the century — for instance, in May 1900, the first ascent of the

*S.M.C.J. Vol. 11, No. 61, p. 22.
†H.F. & G. Witherby, London.

direct route up the celebrated Crowberry Ridge on Buachaille Etive Mor. The Crowberry had in fact been climbed five years earlier, by Naismith and Douglas, but their route had avoided frontal assault by choosing a tamer gully alternative; the face of the superb 750-foot ridge was still waiting. Baker's companions were J.W. Puttrell and the renowned Lake District climbers, the brothers George and Ashley Abraham, and everything went triumphantly well. The long minutes needed for the crux of the climb — the severe traverse from what became known as 'Abraham's Ledge' — must have been packed taut with suspense:

> Here the hardest part of the climb begins, about seventy feet of open face, nearly vertical, and almost destitute of good holds, the few that exist being shallow and sloping the wrong way, so that to stick to the rock at all calls for a sustained effort in balancing. It is a place that makes equal demands on a leader's caution and audacity.
>
> At this point there was a general unroping, for the usual forty feet between each pair of men was quite inadequate for the great pitch. George Abraham led up in brilliant style. Anxiously we watched him quit the platform, stepping out upon a tiny ledge with his left toe, and, moving cautiously leftward and gradually up, disappear from our sight. The rope went out by inches, and we waited in dead silence for a shout to say that the distant platform was won. The shout was a long time coming. At length, the eighty-footer was nearly all paid out, and then the welcome cry came from above with a summons to the next man. And now, with a pause for photography, there was another wait, but this time no need for suspense. Next the rope-end was flung down for the camera, and then my own turn came. Just at the beginning of the critical seventy feet, a shallow saucer-hold, breast-high, sloping out and not affording any grip, is the only fulcrum for lifting the body up four and a half feet vertical. Situations no less trying occur repeatedly. The rocks were firm and solid; but all the way up, in fumbling for finger-holds or a toe-scrape, one had a thrilling view straight down of crags and snowy gullies and precipitous slopes, whilst a bulky rucksack pulling backwards almost outweighed the moral encouragement of the rope.

Higher up, as the climbers cleared the ledges of loose unstable rocks, they dislodged one on to a huge pinnacle below them.

> George Abraham had inspected the pinnacle on our first attempt to get up, but had found it shaky. We calculated afterwards, very moderately I think, that it would weigh eighty or ninety tons, the same practically as a heavy locomotive and tender. The falling rock hit the top of it. The pinnacle shook in its socket, lurched forward, bowed

majestically over, and, almost before we knew what was happening, went hurtling down the cliffs and gullies. It cleared some hundreds of feet at a leap; then, striking a projection, bounded off, leaving an ugly scar behind, and thundered on down the crags, smashing off corners, crashing into the screes in the gullies, and splashing up the snow like water. In a few moments a storm of fragments was flying down the mountain-side, but we could see only the stones that rebounded above the dense cloud of dust. The whole ridge vibrated like a bridge with a heavy express rushing over, and we clung to the rocks with all our nerves tense, wondering if the shock would bring down more pinnacles about our ears.

The year after the Crowberry Ridge epic Baker found himself involved in an even more exciting — though rather less glorious — adventure, this time on the steep granite 'boiler-plates' of the hills of Arran. His friend Puttrell was with him again, and for their delectation another friend, L.J. Oppenheimer, who was holidaying on the island, had chosen a repulsive-looking chimney furrowing the fierce wall of slabs on the east face of Beinn Nuis. Two wives and Oppenheimer's brother formed a party of camp followers who, with greater wisdom, were able to watch the afternoon's proceedings from the safety of the nearby hillside. The day was fine, although previous heavy rain had fallen, making their gully noisy with the music of a mountain burn. The first pitch, a water-slide of some thirty-five feet, gave the trio a foretaste of what lay ahead: it was only with the greatest difficulty and the use of combined tactics — a human pyramid of three — that Puttrell led it, as "all the while the diverted stream was running through our comrade's clothes and bubbling out at his boots." Steep, crumbling rock took the climbers into a gloomy recess, a cave with a roof of gigantic blocks, and once again it was only after a tough struggle that they surmounted the wickedly slippery walls. When apparently harder obstacles confronted them higher up, two-thirds of the party were for retreat, only to have their leader achieve another almost miraculous advance. But the situation was becoming increasingly desperate, each pitch seeming harder than the one before, with descent just not to be contemplated. Eventually, after some particularly hair-raising moves on the crumbling vegetation of the face — by Baker himself as the lightest of the trio — they decided to give in and shouted to the onlookers to go down to Brodick for a rescue party. They had, however, been in the chimney for six hours and the prospect of a wait of several more, soaked to the skin, wretchedly cold and "as hungry as wolves", was so unattractive that Baker was inspired to lead the final seventy feet to easier ground and safety.

Later, on their way down to the glen, they met the rescue party coming up, carrying lanterns, a long rope and brandy. "The brandy," Baker commented, "came from a farm down the glen, and the farmer, we were told, though of the weaker sex, was man enough to promise us a horse-whipping as soon as she set eyes on us. No doubt we richly deserved it."

So far as is known, the Beinn Nuis chimney was not climbed again for another fifty-four years.

The two Abraham brothers, George and Ashley, who had been Ernest Baker's rope companions on the Crowberry Ridge, were quick to note the wonderful scope that existed for breaking new ground and both seized their chances with enthusiasm. George Abraham even went so far as to spend his honeymoon in Glencoe in the October following his Crowberry triumph and he and his wife had some good days, mainly on Bidean nam Bian and its outliers. Winifred's Pinnacle, in the spectacular west-facing Amphitheatre of Aonach Dubh, aptly commemorates their successes. The brothers did a great deal to popularise mountaineering early on in the century, with both their books and their photographs, Ashley Abraham's *Rock Climbing in Skye* making particularly enthralling reading. The steep Cioch Direct climb which he and H. Harland did in 1907 — a popular 'mild severe' of 400 feet — is probably the best known of the Skye achievements he describes.

From end to end of the seven-mile sickle of the Cuillin Ridge new discoveries were made in the years preceding the First World War — some of outstanding character, some of minor interest, but all stressing over and over again the supreme enjoyment of the rough Skye gabbro.

By far the most prominent of the trail-breakers at that time were Dr Guy Barlow, a research physicist at Birmingham University, and his great climbing companion E.W. Steeple, a founder member of the Midland Association of Mountaineers. These two in partnership and often also with other friends contributed an impressively long list of new routes before the war and almost exactly as many more immediately after, when they were busy editing that classic guide-book of the S.M.C., *The Island of Skye*, published in 1923. This book belonged, of course, to a more leisurely era, to a time when notes could be intriguingly expansive, unlike the terse, business-like descriptions of today. (One reads for instance how the pioneers of the west ridge of Sgurr nan Gillean, brought up short by the forbidding-looking gendarme, paused and "smoked a pipe over it" before swinging round it to the narrow edge beyond.) For those climbers who were, so to speak, brought up to know every move and hold on buttress and face and gully-wall almost by heart there was inexhaustible reading for days of enforced idleness in rain-battered tent or among the earwigs on the floor of Macrae's barn in Glen Brittle.

It was on 10th June 1911 that the Cuillin Ridge was first followed in its entirety from Gars-bheinn to Sgurr nan Gillean, a traverse which involves some 10,000 feet of ascent and altogether about fifteen miles of walking and climbing between Glen Brittle and Sligachan. The two climbers to achieve this *tour de force* were L.G. Shadbolt and A.C. McLaren. Leaving Glen Brittle at 3.35 a.m., they reached Gars-bheinn at 6.5, Sgurr Alasdair at 9.0 and the Inaccessible Pinnacle of Sgurr Dearg, well ahead of schedule, at 10.55. Here the mist which had seemed threatening early on cleared completely before a gentle north wind, leaving the sky almost cloudless. The ensuing succession of tops to Bidein Druim nan Ramh presented no serious problems; surprisingly the next section was trickier than expected. As Shadbolt afterwards described it:

> Bruach na Frithe looked very near, and the ridge between us and it deceptively easy, but we found on closer inspection many unsuspected difficulties in the shape of narrow faults generally undercut and usually necessitating a descent slightly on the Coruisk side. One of these has a conspicuous cairn on the edge of a forty-foot overhang, presumably erected by some climber to commemorate the fact that he did not fall over this deceptive place; or, possibly, it is merely a negative cairn marking the way not to go. This portion of the ridge, to be fully appreciated, should, I think, be visited for the first time in thick weather;

it would then afford endless excitement, and strain the resources of the largest bump of locality.*

Tiredness and thirst were beginning to have their effect on the two climbers, but a fine lead by McLaren took them up Naismith's route on the Bhasteir Tooth. Sgurr nan Gillean was reached at 6.25 p.m. and Sligachan, after a wearisome plod down to the glen, at 8.25. "The mind, released from the problems of the immediate future, soon began to recall the incidents of the day, and before Sligachan was reached we had thrilled again to all the delights and doubts of one of the best days we had ever spent together on the hills."

Shadbolt and McLaren climbed in partnership in other parts of Scotland besides Skye, and it is quite remarkable how often one comes across a 'Shadbolt's Chimney' or a 'McLaren's Chimney'. It is well to be reminded so pleasantly of their contributions to the story of Scottish mountaineering.

One other notable milestone before the outbreak of the 1914-18 war falls to be mentioned — the formation of the Ladies' Scottish Climbing Club. In 1907 the first British mountaineering club for women, the Ladies' Alpine Club, had been founded, mainly through the efforts of the celebrated Mrs Aubrey Le Blond. Then in April of the following year the Scottish club was started. The originators of the latter were Mrs William Inglis Clark, her daughter Mabel and Miss Lucy Smith, perhaps not surprisingly a trio with strong S.M.C. connections: Lucy Smith's father had been president in 1902-04, Mrs Inglis Clark's husband, Dr William Inglis Clark, was to hold similar office during the years of the First World War, and her daughter's future husband, Robert Jeffrey, was to be president during the Second World War.

The actual formation of the club took place, appropriately enough, in the lee of a large boulder at Lix, near Killin, following a few days' spring mountaineering on the hills near by. Those were the days, of course, when women's climbing was looked on as something eccentric, if nothing worse. Old photographs show the voluminous skirts and vast hats, anchored occasionally by motoring veils, which must have added enormously to the difficulties of any climb, and it is

*S.M.C.J. Vol. 11, No. 66, p. 328.

hilariously on record how the wearers used often to leave the offending garments hidden under rocks once they were discreetly out of sight. And yet, however amusing that may be, it has its symbolic side too: this triumph over obstacles almost as real in those days as actual rock and ice, no doubt foreshadowed the determination and keenness which has taken later generations of club members to every corner of the Scottish hills, to Wales and the Lake District, to the Alps and Norway, to Greenland and the Himalayas.

9
The Years Between

When one looks back to the youthful, almost ingenuous enthusiasm which characterised the early days of mountaineering in Scotland, or, still more, when one considers the restless, rousing activity in evidence everywhere on the hills today, it is difficult not to dismiss the period of the nineteen-twenties as insipid and undistinguished, disappointingly lacking in enterprise.

Probably those Scots who were active in the years immediately following the First World War would deny indignantly that things were quiet. But the fact is that remarkably little pioneering was done, and that little mainly by non-Scottish visitors. In Skye, for instance, it was the English who held the stage as peace took over from war, most of the names which appear in the records of that time being those of climbers illustrious in the Lake District and Wales. One of the most prominent was George Leigh-Mallory, who was then at the height of his powers and who was destined to make inspiring history on Everest in 1924. The S.M.C's *Guide to the Island of Skye*, the first covering the Cuillin to be published as a separate volume, appeared in 1923, but even that seemed to have no great stimulus except for the joint editors themselves, E.W. Steeple and Guy Barlow, who lost no time in rendering their own work out of date.

Recalling later her first memorable visit to Skye, Miss Dorothy Pilley (later Mrs I.A. Richards) described an encounter with Steeple and Barlow after she and her companions had completed a fine new route, the Cioch West climb:

> The new climb seemed to us rather harder, on the whole, than the Cioch Direct. We noticed at the top that Steeple and Barlow had watched our proceedings and it was kind of them to break through their polite reserve far enough to remark that our climb was 'Very pretty'. Later they thawed so far as to entertain us, with the uttermost hospitality, in Mary Campbell's once famous den. This was a rival

establishment, frequented only by the most courageous at Glen Brittle, a dark cabin with cupboard-like, shut beds in the walls. Here when a large meal ended, tea and eggs in dozens would appear. But Steeple and Barlow beat this. Not content with the tea and eggs in surplus, their hospitality produced a plum pudding boiled in their own billy. It had been gurgling therein succulently all through the meal. Whether it had come to Glen Brittle in one of their locally notorious parcels or had been somehow created by them there I never knew. These parcels were nicely calculated not to exceed either in weight or dimensions the maximum allowed by the Post Office Regulations and yet not to fall short of it. They were elegantly encased in a distinctive buff-coloured material and soundly stitched. You could recognise them a long way off. In a stream of such parcels their entire luggage, gear and provisionment would arrive, harbingers appearing some considerable time before Steeple and Barlow themselves. The feelings of the postman, confronted daily with the largest and weightiest parcel he had yet seen that was just *not* beyond the legal limit, may be imagined. The distance to Glen Brittle is nine miles.*

Elsewhere in Scotland the story was much the same as in Skye. For ten years Ben Nevis was largely neglected, even although the first guide to it was published in 1919, the only real 'classic' being the first winter ascent of Observatory Ridge in early April 1920 by a party under the leadership of Harold Raeburn. Some desultory attacks on the rocks of the western Cairngorms, a more notable campaign on Lochnagar which began in 1927, and a scattering of skirmishes in Glencoe made up the total, more or less, for a decade which was even referred to later as the 'Dark Ages'.

The twenties nevertheless were not entirely without promise; there were one or two immensely encouraging pointers to better things ahead. For example the formation, in 1925, of the Junior Mountaineering Club of Scotland.

In the course of a holiday in the Alps a small party of S.M.C. members had hit on the singularly happy idea of founding this secondary club, mainly to help those who were keen but who had little or no mountaineering experience, and in this way to act as a 'feeder' for the parent body. It was decided initially to start sections in Edinburgh and Glasgow, the first joint meet being held at Crianlarich the following New Year. Enthusiasm grew quickly. Edinburgh to begin with was strongest numerically and even the Perth section,

*Climbing Days by Dorothy Pilley (G. Bell, London, 1935), pp. 101-2.

which was formed early on, took a marginal lead over Glasgow — a state of affairs which, however, was very soon reversed. In 1938 an Inverness branch was added and in 1939 the London section — far from the hills admittedly, but never lacking in ingenuity. There was even one J.M.C.S. member who, in the mid-thirties, claimed to have started a Pekin branch, doing his climbing in Upper Mongolia at weekends. By the start of the war the membership total had risen to 225.

While the name was thoroughly appropriate in the early days and while the J.M.C.S. still regularly provides first-rate new members for the senior club, 'junior' has tended over the years to be a slightly inaccurate description. Often enough members have expressed a healthy impatience — both in deed and in word — with the stick-in-the-mud lack of enterprise of their elders, conveniently forgetting of course the wise dictum of one S.M.C. president and Himalayan veteran that "The tigers of today are the toothless tigers of tomorrow." Nevertheless J.M.C.S. achievements have contributed to a quite remarkable extent to the making of mountaineering history all over the world, from the *Nordwände* of the Alps to the Himalayas, from Arctic Norway and Greenland to some of the toughest problems of South America. Those enthusiasts on holiday back in 1925 could hardly have foreseen what a vigorous youngster they were about to bring into being.

Another particularly outstanding event of the twenties was the building of the Charles Inglis Clark memorial hut high in the Allt a' Mhuilinn glen at the foot of the northern precipices of Ben Nevis. The story of how the idea of erecting a hut there was originally conceived, was interestingly told by Dr Ernest Maylard, one of the original members of the S.M.C.

It was at a dinner in the Alexandra Hotel, Fort William, connected with an Easter Meet, that I ventilated the proposal for the construction of a hut, and my reason for doing so arose in this way. I was wandering up the old path to the summit of the Ben. On arriving at the half-way refuge I found it occupied by two junior members of the Club who were away at the time, but had left all their belongings for a day and a night's lodging. The rotten wooden building was in a wretched condition, absolutely unfit to be occupied by any human beings. As a medical man I could not but admire the enthusiasm of these two junior mountaineers, that they were willing to undergo such discomforts in the pursuit of their pleasure; but at the same time I recognised the risk they were running in damaging their health for future days by sleeping in such a hovel with wet and wind creeping through innumerable crevices. At the dinner I spoke to those seated near me of the need for a properly constructed hut. Sitting at the side of our esteemed and indefatigable secretary Sang, was the factor of the Ben Nevis Estates, as his guest. To these two, seated some little distance away, I went and stated what I have just narrated above regarding the need of a hut. The suggestion was warmly received, and the factor said he would do all he could to help on the project should its inception mature. The next step was to ascertain how and where the money was to be got, for the conveyance of material and the construction of a building far from the supply both of men and material demanded very serious consideration. The thought occurred to me that it might be constructed as a memorial to one or more of our comrades who had lost their lives as the result of the war. There was one outstanding loss which the Club had sustained, and that the only son of one of our most beloved past Presidents, a distinguished climber and a good companion. So I wrote to Inglis Clark, making the suggestion that perhaps the need as well as the personal association might appeal to him. To my great joy he almost at once replied that he and his wife would erect a hut to the memory of their son. I need add nothing further to the subject, but merely state what an inexpressible boon it has been to those who wish to tackle the steep ridges and gullies on the north-east face of the Ben.*

The plan went ahead. Permission for the erection of the hut was duly received on 28th July 1927 and ten months later the first load of materials was carried up. Opening day was 1st April 1929.

Prior to the hut dinner which was laid on to celebrate the occasion, the Rev. A.E. Robertson had asked a blessing and prayed that the building might be a refuge in time of danger. Almost as if to symbolise the invaluable part that the hut was destined to play in countless Nevis rescues in years to come, two climbers came bursting in, exhausted after a fall high in Observatory Gully. They had been swept down for some 600 feet, and seeing a light in the hut window had made their way to it. Fortunately after a rest and tea they were able to continue on their way down to Fort William.

As we move on to the background to the early thirties, it is perhaps worth recalling that in those days the roads in the Highlands were still remarkably poor; not quite so daunting admittedly as in the heyday of those ubiquitous pioneers of the north-west, W.N. Ling and G.T. Glover, but none the less

*S.M.C.J. Vol. 22, No. 127, pp. 12-13.

The eastern corrie of Stob Coir' an Albannaich, Glen Etive

Gleouraich (3,395 feet), a fine hill on the north side
of Loch Quoich, Inverness-shire

April sun on the hills to the south-west of Loch Quoich

utterly deplorable by modern standards. It was only in 1933, and even then despite a storm of antagonism which had been rumbling and grumbling for years, that the present road through Glencoe was opened, replacing the jolly switchback of grassy corners and hump-backed bridges which had served for so long before that. Other roads, equally important, were as ludicrous — or as tragic — with single-track running the rule far more often than the exception. At Strome Ferry the old Alligin-built boat, side-decked and capable of carrying only one car, did service until July 1938, and at Dornie it was not until the war that the present bridge across the tide-race of Loch Long was opened; indeed, a journey to Skye could well be a nightmare experience indelibly impressed on the memory: the appalling rutted and potholed 'track' via Tomdoun and Cluanie and down Glen Shiel, the two tortoise-crossings at Dornie and Kyle, and finally the nine miles, rough as a stream-bed and as deadly for car-springs and sumps, to journey's end in Glen Brittle itself. Even at the end of the day, a really good base for the Cuillin Ridge used to be a perennial problem. The comparative luxury of hut and hostel and the orientation of the Glen Brittle folk towards mass camping belonged entirely to the future. It was permissible to pitch a tent anywhere one chose — and some of the choices could be odd to say the least — but Skye weather being what it is, and Highland cattle having notorious appetites for almost any variety of tent-fabric, many a retreat had to be beaten to the welcome sanctuary of Macrae's barn. Enthusiasm had to be proof against many tribulations — certainly not forgetting the midges.

Yet not for worlds would we have had things any different, those of us who remember those days that are past when first we discovered the delights of rock and snow, ridge and corrie. There was a sense of fun and adventure and discovery which, for all the advanced techniques and high standards of today, has inevitably departed, in part at least, with the coming of easy travel and better accommodation.

Some of the cheeriest pages in the whole story of the Scottish hills could well be written round Inverarnan Hotel, the tall white roadside building so familiar to motorists crossing the little Dunbartonshire-Perthshire boundary bridge where the Loch Lomond flats finally end and the climb up Glen Falloch begins. At Inverarnan, over a period of close on forty years, the kindness and hospitality of the Girvan family, the owners, became nothing less than legendary. Three generations of climbers, hill-walkers and skiers came to know and value a welcome there as warm and as true as any to be found north of the Border. In winter and spring especially the Girvans' own fireside — remembered affectionately as 'the den' — became the happiest of meeting-places for lively conversation and all the news of the hills; at New Year the song and story and good cheer among old friends became a traditional item of the mountaineering calendar. When, in 1966, winter closing became necessary, there was nowhere else comparable to turn to and when, four years later, the hotel was sold and Nancy and Hannah Girvan went north to live at Invergarry, they left a blank that was quite impossible to fill.

Back in the bleak days of the depression, however, there were plenty of youngsters who quite simply had no money at all to spend on such luxuries as a roof and a bed. On Clydeside especially, where shipbuilding was at a standstill, times were desperately hard; throughout Central Scotland unemployment was widespread. It was therefore in the nature of things that more and more of those with time hanging heavily on their hands should find compensation in escape to the hills from the grey tenements and silent yards. Nor were their discoveries limited to the joys of the peaks themselves. They perfected the technique of living rough, sleeping sometimes in barns or deserted cottages, sometimes in caves or laboriously constructed 'howffs' under giant sheltering boulders as often as not without such soft refinements as sleeping-bags or blankets. The exploits of these hardy souls would fill a book — and a good one at that: discovering for example, as one account has it, that porridge made from icicles tastes much better than porridge made from snow; wakening up on a New Year's morning to hear half a dozen sets of teeth chattering in unison, or scooping rocks from an uneven floor with no tools other than flattened soup-tins. Some of the best 'howffs' were located in the Arrochar hills, for example at the well-known Narnain Stone, or in the lower corrie of The Brack, above Glen Croe. Further afield, Glencoe ranked almost as high on the list, with such obvious bivouacking terrain as the jaws of the Lost Valley; in the Cairngorms the Shelter Stone of Loch Avon, able to sleep some eight to ten, had been in the five-star category from the days of the old-time freebooters.

Three clubs came into being in those spartan days — the Ptarmigan Club, restricted to sixteen members, in 1929, the Creagh Dhu Mountaineering Club in 1930, and the Lomond Mountaineering Club, founded in 1933. Not surprisingly much of their attention was focussed on the Arrochar hills as being the nearest good playground to the main industrial centres. Almost suddenly, after a quarter of a century's neglect, The Cobbler was discovered to be a mountain of many possibilities. Fired by a fresh enthusiasm, the new pioneers opened up whole areas previously classed as unclimbable on both South and North Peaks. A good dozen new routes, almost all of a high standard of difficulty, gave the rock-climbing records a wholly original look and pointed the way to still harder possibilities for the future, possibilities which have been fully exploited since the end of the war, mainly by members of the Creagh Dhu Club.

The spirit of those remarkable, adventurous pre-war days was captured to perfection by Alastair Borthwick in his classic, *Always a Little Further** — the kind of book to which one returns again and again for a good jog to the memory and unlimited quiet chuckles. There is in it indeed such a vast store of humour, whether it be in descriptions of the questionable pleasures of mountaineering discomforts, in pictures of beginners' blunderings, or in anecdotes expressive of the sheer zest of youthful dare-devilry, that in a way it is ageless. And yet the characters for the most part, met with and relished to the full in bivouac or barn, in fair weather or in foul, could belong only to the inventive, poverty-stricken thirties.

This new, democratic spirit of the hills was not, however, something which petered out with the return of a modicum of prosperity to Scotland, although in some ways it changed in

*Most recent edition, John Smith, Glasgow, 1969.

character. After the war there was an even greater and a growing urge among young people to 'escape' at week-ends, to get away from the towns to enjoy the open spaces to the full. Equipment now was better, partly because money was not quite so scarce, partly because of the ex-Army kit that was available at cheap prices; rucksacks and tents, anoraks and sleeping-bags made their appearance more often among the lively parties who 'hitched' or set off by bus Friday evening after Friday evening to Aberfoyle or the Trossachs, the Black Mount or Glencoe. Yet the mood was no less carefree, the repartee and the music gave access no less freely to a cheery world of its own. A great respect for the countryside was taken for granted, as too was a knowledge of every stick and stone of the familiar routes summer and winter, year in year out. Those who 'padded' the well-known paths with their mountainous rucksacks and their guitars still tell of visits to Ben Alder cottage carrying only potatoes and turnips and onions as supplies, but with a venison fry-up in prospect; of night walks to the lonely bothy far up Glen Strae, or to Glasahoile above the shore of Loch Katrine; of 'drumming up' at friendly camp-sites like the forest clearing near Ba Bridge or, not so far from home in the Aberfoyle hills, the 'La-di-dah' or the 'Shangri La'.

It was also during the thirties, of course, that the youth hostelling movement was started in Scotland and gained momentum at almost unbelievable speed. The hostelling idea had in fact been born many years before, in 1909, when a German schoolmaster, Richard Schirrmann, hit on the plan of using schools during holiday periods to accommodate children from industrial areas and introduce them to the beauties of the countryside. Schirrmann's own school at Altena, in Westphalia, became the first youth hostel. The success which followed this experiment in Germany duly inspired a number of enthusiasts in Scotland to follow suit and, thanks to their efforts, a public meeting was held in Edinburgh on 13th February, 1931, at which the Scottish Youth Hostels Association was born.

The chief object then, as now, was "To help all, but especially young people of limited means living and working in industrial and other areas to know, use, and appreciate the

Scottish countryside and places of historic and cultural interest in Scotland, and to promote their health, recreation and education, particularly by providing simple hostel accommodation for them on their travels."

The first Scottish hostel to be opened was Broadmeadows, in the Borders, on the banks of Yarrow Water between St Mary's Loch and Selkirk. The developments which followed exceeded all expectations, so that by 1936 there were no less than forty-eight hostels, with the Association's membership approaching 12,000. In the many years since those early ventures, changes have taken place: the size of hostels has tended to become greater; meals are now provided in some; grading has been introduced. Yet for the most part the basic hostelling principles of self cooking and simple accommodation have been retained, a policy reflected in the modern figures — of 1973, for example, when there were eighty hostels providing over half a million bednights to members of the forty-seven countries within the International Youth Hostel Federation.

The movement, obviously, has played a vital part in the opening up of the Scottish hills. Hostels like Loch Ossian and Glen Affric provide magnificent bases for 'escape' to some of the wildest country in the Highlands; the Glendoll hostel, says the handbook, offers "Many fine circular walks. Thirty peaks of over 3,000 feet in this area;" Glencoe and Glenbrittle, Glen Nevis and Loch Morlich speak for themselves. There is no end to the opportunities up and down the country. In addition these days a splendid selection of 'adventure' courses is open to youngsters — sailing and canoeing, angling and ski-ing, pony-trekking and field studies, orienteering and gliding. Both general mountaineering and more specialised climbing have important places in the programmes, with invitations to novices and — especially in Skye on Sron na Ciche and elsewhere on the main Guillin Ridge — to those with some rock-climbing experience to work up to routes of temptingly higher standards.

Of immense significance to all with the best interests of the Highlands at heart, and indeed to all future generations as well, was the acquisition by the National Trust for Scotland of the two neighbouring estates of Glencoe and Dalness. These

came up for sale in 1935 and 1937 and, in great measure
through the financial help given by the S.M.C., the other
mountaineering clubs and the Pilgrim Trust, were handed
over to the National Trust for Scotland to be held in
perpetuity for the nation. This meant that at all times in the
future there would be free and unrestricted access to some of
the finest climbing and walking country in the Highlands,
including all the 'tops' of Buachaille Etive Mor, Buachaille
Etive Beag and Bidean nam Bian on the south side of the glen
and, on the north side, the whole magnificent saw-edge ridge
of the Aonach Eagach. Over and above this, in 1972, the Trust
purchased the 1,390 acre farm of Achnacon from the Forestry
Commission. Astride the main A82 immediately to the west of
the previous boundary, this new property gives much needed
protection to an additional important part of the Glencoe
landscape and has allowed also for the establishment of a base
for research in mountain safety techniques and rescue work.
The main scene of the Massacre is the site of the present
village of Glencoe and is not in fact Trust property. On the
other hand, Signal Rock, once an outlook post of the
Macdonalds, is within the Trust's boundaries, as is the
familiar landmark of Ossian's Cave, high on the north face of
Aonach Dubh.

On 20th July 1937 a particularly interesting event took
place — the revival after a lapse of thirty-four years of the Ben
Nevis race. This famous marathon — supreme test of fitness,
mental as well as physical — really dates back to 1895 when
William Swan, a Fort William hairdresser, ran to the summit
and back in the remarkable time of 2 hours 41 minutes. His
starting-point was the old post office in the Fort William High
Street and as a new office had been opened before another
attempt was made two years later, his record has remained
unbeaten. Competition was fierce, however: in 1897 a Colonel
Spencer Acklom of the Connaught Rangers, aged fifty-three,
set a time for the new course of 2 hours 55 minutes, only to
have this beaten the following year by a Leith athlete, W.
MacDonald, and beaten again after only a couple of months
by the original stalwart Willie Swan. In these early days there
were several variations — a race from Banavie, for instance, in
which ten competitors took part, and in 1903 a race from

Achintee farm to the summit only. This latter event was won by the observatory roadman Ewan McKenzie, who also won the official contest later that same year. In this unfortunately one of the contestants collapsed and remained unconscious for ten hours, a fact which, together with the closing of the observatory the following year, probably led to the race being discontinued. It is strange nevertheless that it was not revived until 1937.

In 1943 the starting-point was changed from the post office to the King George V playing field on account of the increasingly heavy traffic in the town; then in 1971 it was moved yet again to the New Town Park not far from the entrance to Glen Nevis. Almost unbelievably the record — by H.D. Walker of Blackburn Harriers in 1973 — now stands at 1 hour 29 minutes 38 seconds. The popularity of the event may be gauged by the fact that individual entrants for the contest can number over 200, with almost a score of teams competing for special trophies. To cope with this 'invasion' elaborate organisation is needed, especially as even in the best of summers the weather on the Ben can vary enormously; thus in 1937 one reads "Conditions ideal except for mist on the summit"; in 1939, "Misty and heavy going"; in 1952, "Conditions: blizzard on summit. Wet and cold from half-way down. Nine competitors retired".

Interestingly enough, records on the Ben have not belonged exclusively to the men. The best women's time from the post office to the summit was achieved back in 1909, when Miss Elizabeth Wilson-Smith, of Duns, Berwickshire, made the ascent in 1 hour 51 minutes. Then almost half a century later, in 1955, sixteen-year-old Kathleen Connochie, daughter of a Fort William doctor, set up a time of 3 hours 2 minutes for the return run from the King George V playing field — a truly remarkable achievement.

Ben Nevis, of course, is an essential component of the 'Motorised Three Peaks' marathon, the endurance test which involves visiting the highest points in Wales, England and Scotland. To illustrate the toughness and hot pace demanded for this, mention may be made of the performance of a four-man Vauxhall Motors team who achieved a record-breaking 13 hours 43 minutes in June 1973. Started at 3 a.m. by the

Mayor of Caernarvon, they had two enthusiasts waiting at the top of Snowdon to witness their arrival, a noted fell runner to guide them up and down Scafell Pike in poor visibility, speedboats to set them swiftly across Loch Leven at Ballachulish and, not surprisingly, plenty of local support to encourage them on the last lap up and down the Ben. The individual record for this feat incidentally is held at present by Joss Naylor, of Kendal — an almost incredible 11 hours 52 minutes.

Looking back now to the years between the two world wars, it is difficult to see why, relatively speaking, actual climbing achievements on the Scottish hills were so limited. Inevitably, of course, there had to be a period of recovery after 1918, but this could not really be continued as a valid excuse far beyond the twenties. There was certainly no lack of inspiration in the pattern of mountaineering and exploration abroad: 1924 and 1933, for example, were great years in the epic of Everest; Frank Smythe was writing of notable achievements in the Alps — one thinks especially of his famous routes with Graham Brown on the Brenva face of Mont Blanc; Gino Watkins and his outstanding group of companions were making exploration history on the east coast of Greenland; Kamet and Nanda Devi, Nanga Parbat and Kangchenjunga had become familiar names with familiar stories; the first north-face nationalism, much of it glorifying Hitler, was shaping a new — and notorious — pattern of heroics on the very verge of the impossible on the Eiger, the Matterhorn and the Grandes Jorasses.

Nor indeed was there any lack of keenness at home. How determined, for instance, was that small band of enthusiasts to solve one of 'the Buachaille's' most intriguing problems of those days — the discovery of a way up the Rannoch Wall, the alluring, formidable eastern flank of the Crowberry Ridge! And what jubilation there was on that June day in 1934 when they finally opened up Route I — let it be added, without any mechanical aids. None of the party of four on that historic first climb can have had any inkling of the popularity that the Wall would achieve later through the addition of another dozen or so routes and variations close by, of which Agag's Groove, climbed two years after Route I, has come to be much the most frequented.

One of the original Rannoch Wall quartet, Dr G. Graham Macphee, was about that time particularly deeply involved in the climbing, both summer and winter, on Ben Nevis. A dentist with a busy practice in Liverpool, Macphee undertook the compilation of a new edition of the S.M.C. guide to Ben Nevis, duly published in 1936, although this entailed an almost endless succession of week-end round trips each of some 600 miles. When one pauses to consider just exactly what this meant, it is not quite so easy to pass judgment on those days as lacking seriously in enthusiasm. It was Macphee's regret that he had insufficient opportunities to do all the known climbs himself, but he was not far from achieving this ideal, and into the bargain he accomplished a notable amount of individual pioneering. A number of fine routes, such as the winter ascent of Tower Gap Chimney — a March day of fourteen hours from the Charles Inglis Clark hut — and in summer on the Trident buttresses are among the achievements which bear the stamp of his genius. Winter climbing especially owed much to Macphee's lead in the thirties, although good work was done on the Ben by others as well, summer and winter, among the most outstanding efforts being Sandy Wedderburn's classic Slav Route, followed the year after by the first of the great Orion cluster of climbs on the face of the North-East Buttress, territory which was to become very much the preserve of Dr J.H.B. Bell.

Elsewhere in Scotland the records had rather a thin look about them, although one or two areas made up in quality what they lacked in quantity: thus in the Cairngorms there was the remote Mitre Ridge of Beinn a' Bhuird and on Lochnagar Eagle Buttress and Parallel Buttress, all three milestones of interest. Exploration in the islands (apart from Skye) went on intermittently, although what was achieved was of surprisingly little consequence when one considers the discoveries which have been made more recently, for example in the Arran hills, on Rum and in Harris.

Glencoe was in fact the area where successes were most noteworthy. Apart from the face routes on the Rannoch Wall which have been mentioned, three particularly fine gully climbs were achieved, all by Scottish parties — the Chasm and Raven's Gully on Buachaille Etive Mor and Clachaig Gully on the south flank of Sgor nam Fiannaidh at the other end of the glen. Each of these was in its own way an epic achievement, for although the deep 1,400-foot gash of the Chasm had been climbed before, it had lacked an escape from the final fierce difficulty, the Devil's Cauldron, to make it satisfactorily complete; Raven's Gully provided a half-way 'pitch' that was particularly severe for those days, while Clachaig Gully — described as "the longest gully in Britain" — had been attracting the attention of top-class mountaineers since the days of Professor Norman Collie half a century before.

Worthy of mention apart from these classics, the Cuneiform Buttress overlooking Raven's Gully and several new routes on Central Buttress were excellent climbs in themselves and in addition provided interesting keys to quite a number of future discoveries on 'the Buachaille'. Of much the most importance, however, in the years just before the war were the snow and ice climbs which were carried out, mostly in Glencoe, by a small group of climbers outstanding for their initiative and enterprise. The story of these has been told with gripping vividness by W.H. Murray in his two books *Mountaineering in Scotland* and *Undiscovered Scotland**. Murray was responsible both through his writing and through the deeds he described, for inspiring a tremendous resurgence in Scottish climbing; his influence indeed was to be felt for many years. The war put a temporary, abrupt stop to his activities on Highland rock, snow and ice, although fate decreed that as a prisoner-of-war he should have more than ample leisure for setting down his narratives — a mischance for him, if truly fortunate for Scottish mountaineering.

In Skye during the inter-war years astonishingly little of note was achieved. The few first-class new routes which were pioneered were mostly done by English parties, almost all on Sron na Ciche and Sgurr Sgumain. Then out of the blue as it were, in the summer of 1939 within weeks of the outbreak of war, a remarkable feat was performed — strangely enough twice in quick succession — the traverse of the main Cuillin Ridge together with the outlying 'Munro' Blaven and its lesser neighbour Clach Glas. The Ridge itself, it will be recalled,

*Dent, 1947 and 1951.

had been traversed in its entirety as far back as 1911, but this new *tour de force* — now known as the Greater Traverse — added to the 'normal' 10,000 feet of climbing a drop almost to sea-level and a further 3,000 feet of ascent, thus making the day into a marathon mightily impressive. The first of the two expeditions, in mid-June, was made no easier by a boisterous wind throughout and even intermittent snow-showers between Sgurr Alasdair and Sgurr a' Ghreadaidh; the second, carried out just over two months later, was faster by one hour between the first and last summits — nineteen hours against twenty — a remarkable achievement indeed.

Thus in both Skye and Glencoe the signs of a great new awakening were clear enough immediately before the war. The modest river was about to become a flood. Not surprisingly the actual breakthrough was to be contained — partially at any rate — for the six years of hostilities. Thereafter, with remarkably little delay, the banks were to be well and truly burst by the overwhelming tide of fresh enthusiasm.

10
War-Time Interlude

It is hardly ever recalled nowadays how in the early months of the Second World War, before Dunkirk and even before the tragedy of the Norwegian campaign, bitter fighting raged between Russia and Finland. For many weeks the Finns held out gallantly against the invading Russian 'steamroller', using their skill in reconnaissance and forest warfare to keep their Mannerheim Line intact. The extraordinary courage which they showed evoked sympathy far and wide, and in Britain and France particularly efforts were made — for the most part hopelessly muddled and inefficient — to provide men and materials in support. Eventually, in January and February 1940, a specialist ski-battalion — the 5th (Special Reserve) Scots Guards — was raised as Britain's contribution, and mustered in readiness at Quebec Barracks, Bordon, near Aldershot. Men of many nationalities came forward as volunteers, both from the Forces and from civilian life, to join this remarkable unit, Alpine climbers, Everesters, Greenland explorers, Cresta bob-runners and of course well-known skiers among them. It was perhaps the most unusual and potentially one of the finest Army units ever raised in Britain. Its existence, however, was short-lived. Ten days were spent ski-ing with the Chasseurs Alpins at Chamonix — "ski experts from Scotland" ran the description in one of the then uncensored French papers — after which the whole battalion was brought back to this country and after a night in Glasgow on board the troopship *Batory*, was finally disbanded at Bordon. With a nice touch of irony, only some three weeks later the Germans invaded Narvik and the Norwegian campaign had begun.

A few men of vision, wise in the ways of the mountains, saw clearly the lessons of Chamonix and Norway. Other countries had for long appreciated the value of mountain troops, and in particular that whereas the latter could fight anywhere, ordinary infantry were at a hopeless disadvantage in the hills.

Thus France had her Chasseurs Alpins, Italy her Alpini, Germany her Bergtruppen — all élite troops. And Britain had none, apart that is from the Sikhs and the Gurkhas; in Norway such troops could have been invaluable. Efforts were made to persuade the War Office to remedy the lack without delay.

One man who was particularly keen on this concept was E.A.M. (Sandy) Wedderburn, who lost his life so tragically in Italy in 1944 when second-in-command of the Lovat Scouts. Before the war a Writer to the Signet in Edinburgh, Wedderburn had had immensely wide and varied mountaineering and ski-ing experience, principally in Scotland and the Alps, having taken part in a number of outstanding first ascents such as the Slav Route on Ben Nevis and the Mitre Ridge of Beinn a' Bhuird. A man of unusually imaginative thinking and outstanding powers of leadership, he quickly made his mark in the Army. After serving with the Finnish volunteer ski-battalion, he was commissioned in the Royal Scots, then from the summer of 1940 onwards until November 1943, when he joined the Lovats, he held various appointments with Combined Operations. To some extent these bore out his recommendations regarding snow and mountain warfare, even taking him overseas for spells in Iceland and the United States. One interesting command he was given was that of No. 14 Commando, a unit intended specially for mountain operations; as C.O. he had several famous mountaineers under him, and some preparatory training was actually carried out in the Cairngorms, but — one imagines much to his disappointment — the unit never approached full strength and eventually was disbanded.

For some time while he was with Combined Ops, Wedderburn was stationed at the Special Training Centre at Lochailort, some fifteen miles from Mallaig, one of the many places tucked away in the Highlands where strange things went on in those very early days of our war-time fight-back. The Prince Charlie country round Lochailort was, of course, ideal for training purposes, and imaginative exercises took in most of the hills and glens of Morar, Arisaig and Moidart, with, in addition, more ambitious schemes ranging as far afield as Glencoe, the Loch Laggan country and Skye. Speedmarching, living off the country — from berries and nettles to gulls' eggs and rabbits — unarmed combat, bivouacking and numerous other variations all played their parts in making the courses rather more than merely an agreeable change from ordinary Army routine. The pattern they followed owed not a little to Wedderburn's counsels and influenced in turn to some extent the thinking behind much of the mountain warfare training carried out during the later years of the war.

Not many miles from Lochailort and close by the River Arkaig, which forms the mile-long link between Loch Arkaig and Loch Lochy, Achnacarry House had been handed over for the duration to the military authorities by its owner, Sir Donald Cameron of Lochiel. In turn this became the Commando Depot and, later, the Commando Basic Training Centre, where between 1942 and 1945 some 25,000 commando soldiers were trained. In command of the centre was the now legendary Lieutenant Colonel Charles Edward Vaughan, O.B.E., London-born ex R.S.M. in the Guards; under his inescapable eye the stoutest heart was apt to quail, as he saw to it to no mean purpose that some of the toughest, most successful Army training ever devised was carried through day after exacting day, week after exacting week. There are plenty of 'Old Comrades' all over the world who will not readily forget the rain and the mud and the utter weariness, the speed marches and the 'abseils' and the mid-air specialities high above the Arkaig or up in the Achnacarry beeches, most of all perhaps the night assault landings across Loch Lochy, when the hill-slopes overlooking the woods of the Dark Mile echoed and re-echoed to the crackle and whine of small arms fire, the explosions of mortar bombs and the exultant crashes of demolitions.

But although the hills played their part in the tough training at Achnacarry, they were not in any way of major importance. It was not until December 1942 that they came into their own with the formation of a unit more specifically concerned with operations at higher altitudes. Brought into being initially to train commando troops to fight in snow-covered mountain country, this unit was based at Braemar, the first Commanding Officer being Squadron Leader F.S. Smythe, of Everest fame, and the instructors all experienced mountaineers, several with Alpine and Himalayan experience. Numbers 1, 4 and 10 Commandos all participated in the training which — with an eye no doubt to the mountains of German-occupied Norway — ranged far and wide over the plateaux of the Cairngorms and was suitably strenuous and exacting. After several months, however, a new War Office decision decreed that commando troops should not be used in this specialised role, and the unit — now known officially as the Commando Mountain Warfare Training Centre — was given instead the task of training the Lovat Scouts as a mountaineer battalion. In 1943, therefore, a move was made to North Wales, Major G.R. Rees Jones taking over command. There, for some four months of a cold and wet autumn, basic rock-climbing training was carried out. Then, shortly before Christmas, further moves were made: the Lovats were sent out to Canada, where, based on Jasper, they trained further in ski-ing and winter mountaineering before joining in the fighting in Italy; a party of instructors went out to a mountain training school in the Lebanon, and the C.M.W.T.C. itself moved down to Cornwall, where in balmy conditions suggestive of the South of France, three Marine Commandos were trained in cliff-assault techniques prior to D-Day. Following this the unit itself became more specialised in small-boat work and took part in several operations in North-West Europe.

The Army commandos, of course, went out of existence after the war, but it is perhaps worth remembering that not a little of the arduous training carried out and developed in subsequent years by the Royal Marines and other branches of the Services rests on the foundations which they laid. No doubt the snow warfare techniques practised today, in the Cairngorms and elsewhere, have advanced far thanks to the vastly improved equipment; but there is a familiar ring about the calls that are used in standard rock-climbing 'drill', and mountain rescue work still owes much to war-time methods of casualty evacuation.

A simple stone and plaque placed close beside the Forestry Commission's information centre at Glenmore — looking out over the pines to the northern corries of Cairn Gorm — recall another exciting chapter in the history of the war. The memorial is to the Norwegians — officers and men of the Kompani Linge — who lived and trained in the Cairngorms between 1941 and 1945. Composed principally of men who were escaping across the North Sea from German-occupied Norway, the Kompani Linge was welded into a highly efficient unit under the aegis of the Special Operations Executive, the organisation created by the War Cabinet after the fall of France to carry out all kinds of subversive operations in enemy territory. In the Cairngorms the Norwegians found ideal country for living hard and training hard, and were able to carry out many daring attacks, the most important and best known of which was that on the heavy water factory at Vermork, in Telemark, in February, 1943. In the course of these various raids no less than fifty-seven men lost their lives.

On the plaque itself a handsome tribute, in Norwegian as well as in English, is paid to the people of Speyside who gave generous hospitality: "You opened your homes and your hearts to us — and gave us hope."

On a very much larger scale was the training carried out in the Cairngorms by the 52nd (Lowland) Division. In this, amusingly enough, there proved to be a double irony — of a lowland formation being made ready over a period of some three years to operate specifically in the mountains and then, in the event, of its actually having to go into action below sea-level, at the Dutch island of Walcheren. In Scotland the division was spread out over much of the north-east, from the upper reaches of Speyside down to the coast at Aberdeen, some of the time being spent at civilised levels, some less comfortably in the hills. Company courses were run at Dalwhinnie; officers and senior N.C.O.'s were quartered in Glen Feshie; there was a camp site near Loch Pityoulish; in Aviemore the main road seemed never to be free from noise, with Army vehicles clattering through or, almost equally often, the mules of the Indian pack transport and mountain artillery trailing interminably past in one direction or the other.

One obvious part of the division's training programme was ski-ing, and many and wonderful were the trials and tribulations undergone in the course of duty — in the days before such soft options as chairlifts or ski-tows were known

From the roadside near Laxford Bridge, Sutherland: Arkle (2,580 feet) and Loch Stack

Looking north
across the foot
of Glen
Torridon to
Beinn Alligin

April day on the
Aonach Eagach,
Glencoe

on the Scottish hills. Actual ski equipment was not a general issue, but was drawn by those going on what may perhaps be best described as crash courses, whenever snow conditions were suitable. Another favourite pastime was learning the art of glissading, and here again those whose trials on the snow-slopes left indelible scars on memory are certainly not lacking in volubility to describe their experiences. Just how difficult it can be to stop on steep, hard-frozen snow, using a rifle as brake instead of an ice-axe, may well be left to the imagination.

Apart altogether from the Army frolics on and around the hills, there was quite a considerable amount of activity of other kinds going on. Rock-climbing history for one thing, although inevitably slowed down, was not by any means halted.

No doubt in part at least because the hills further afield were out of reach, the buttresses and ridges of Arran came in for a tiger's share of attention. They had in fact been sadly neglected since the early pioneering days, when attacks were put in most notably on the north-east face of Cir Mhor and in the none too attractive chimneys and gullies of Beinn Nuis and Beinn Tarsuinn; thereafter, between the beginning of the century and the outbreak of the Second World War, no more than half a dozen new routes were achieved. Suddenly with the war came a whole crop of interesting discoveries, nearly a score being recorded in the peak years of 1943 and 1944. Fascinating new names such as Caliban's Creep and Prospero's Peril, Pagoda Ridge and Labyrinth appeared to tempt the faithful across to Arran, several of the novelties being routes of real character.

Undoubtedly, however, the finest route on the island — and indeed reckoned to be one of the most satisfying anywhere in Scotland — is the South Ridge Direct of Cir Mhor's Rosa Pinnacle. This justly celebrated climb, first done in the summer of 1941, measures 855 feet, has twelve 'pitches' and is given the classification of 'very severe'. It would be something of an exaggeration to assert that any rock-climb in Scotland enjoys certain sunshine, but at least this route on the Rosa Pinnacle is south-facing and thus catches such sunshine as is going — unlike so many with cold, shadowed outlooks to the north. On a cloudless day of high summer, with the coarse granite almost painfully hot to the touch, the celebrated 'S' crack and, higher, the airy 'lay-back' and delicate slab traverse might perhaps be said to provide the ultimate in rock-climbing satisfaction.

Skye and the Cuillin, being virtually out of bounds in a 'protected area', produced nothing of any note during the war years. Things were better in the Cairngorms, where there was a fair scattering of new climbs, the main concentration — if such it can be called — being on the walls of the great Braeriach-Cairn Toul amphitheatre; on Lochnagar, with the inevitable two or three exceptions, it was not until 1949 that the new era of high-grade snow and ice climbing fairly dawned. Glencoe's contribution was confined almost entirely to Buachaille Etive Mor, and there in particular to problems on the North Buttress and the verticalities of the Rannoch Wall.

Without a doubt, by far the most important advances in the mountaineering sphere were made on the great north-eastern face of Ben Nevis. Between 1942 and 1944 the two-mile line of precipices became almost the exclusive preserve of that brilliant climber B.P. Kellett, who with Miss Nan Forsyth of the Ladies' Scottish Climbing Club tragically lost his life in an accident on Cousins' Buttress on the Ben in September 1944. Kellett made remarkable use of his leisure opportunities while engaged on forestry work in the Fort William area, so much so indeed that his climbing exploits altered dramatically the whole record of achievements on Ben Nevis. In the course of only two short summers he pioneered nearly thirty new routes or variations, half of them either 'severe' or 'very severe' and half, too, done solo. Some of the routes he worked out in the course of his meteoric career fitted into the 'constellation' of climbs on the immense north-west face of the Ben's North-East Buttress, aptly known as the Orion Face. Exploration here had in fact begun in 1935 and had been taken several stages further in the summer of 1940, so that Kellett's achievements added yet again to the interest. These were all without exception summer climbs; now in the years since the war it is this corner of Ben Nevis which has to a notable extent attracted the most enterprising of the snow and ice 'hard men'.

Thus, in many different and unforeseen ways, the war years made their contribution to the changing pattern of the mountain story. New ideas, new equipment, new techniques, new standards, above all new horizons played their own particular parts. Far more men and women than ever before, young and not so young had been introduced to the hills — some to find them cold and unfriendly, even actively hostile; others to decide they were merely something to be put up with. Yet fortunately there were the very many too who discovered in them a new dimension altogether, who knew for sure that they would return to enjoy what they had found. The new, almost incredible expansion was just about to begin.

11

Ski-ing

One of the outdoor pursuits which seems to have been indulged in now and again by the staff of the Ben Nevis observatory was ski-ing. In those days, round about the close of last century, the sport was a novel one in Scotland and, to judge by the descriptions, those who took part in it up on the summit plateau of the Ben — apparently right alongside the ice-fringe of the northern cliffs — must have been singularly lucky to survive. Unfortunately the mists of passing years have blurred exact details of their escapades.

Others, however, were experimenting also round about the same time. In March 1891 W.W. Naismith and a friend climbed Meikle Bin (1,870 feet) in the Campsies from behind Milton and obviously enjoyed themselves immensely. Writing of the outing afterwards, Naismith found it necessary to begin with a word of explanation:

> On the Campsie Fells with Norwegian 'Skis' — For the sake of any uninitiated, it may be explained that skis (*pron. 'shes'*) are wooden snow-skates, 7 feet long and 3 to 4 inches wide, largely used throughout the northern parts of Europe and Asia.*

On the way up the hill the skis were found to be of little value, but during the descent even a slight gradient was sufficient to allow a "tremendous speed" to be reached. Naismith even went the length of commenting that "in the Alps it is not unlikely that the sport may eventually become popular."

Another of the pioneers whose first experience of ski-ing dated from much about the same time as Naismith's, was Harold Raeburn, although oddly enough he was not enthusiastic about possibilities in Scotland. A former president of the S.M.C., Harry MacRobert, describes how Raeburn introduced him to ski-ing in 1905 on the Pentlands, outside Edinburgh:

*S.M.C.J. Vol. 2, No. 1, pp. 89-90.

The ski were long and narrow, with a thong binding, and our efforts were not very successful, although we created some surprise by ski-ing down the tramway lines to Morningside Station on our way home about midnight. Raeburn looked on them entirely from the Norwegian point of view and was not impressed.*

In those early days certainly the emphasis was very strongly Norwegian: interest was focused on Langlauf rather than on downhill running. Thus, when the Scottish Ski Club was founded in 1907, the first honorary member was Dr Fridtjof Nansen, and in the letter which was written to him thanking him for accepting this membership the writer stated: "The formation of the Scottish Ski Club is the latest phase in the movement which was started by the publication of your book describing the 'First Crossing of Greenland'."

By 1909 another S.M.C. member, Allan Arthur, who was also a great ski-enthusiast, was able to write:

The sport of ski-ing has come to stay . . . As a rule, I use two sticks, the one being a strong bamboo pole about 6 feet 6 inches long, with an iron spike and 3-inch plate at one end, and the other, a light bamboo one, with swivel pig-skin basket at the foot for support on the snow.†

Arthur was able to recall many good days on the Perthshire hills, on the Monadh Liath, on Ben Nevis and elsewhere. He even describes how he had "another excellent day in March, going down to Bridge of Weir by a morning train, putting on ski there, and journeying via Queen's Hill (1,673 feet) and Misty Law (1,663 feet) to Lochwinnoch, a distance of about eighteen miles, and thence back by train."**

Particularly notable in the early days was the meet of the S.M.C. at Aviemore at Easter 1913, when an unusually large number of keen skiers were present. Conditions were just right, with ideal snow and lavish sunshine. The accent was, of course, still strongly on cross-country expeditions, one party crossing from Glenmore over Cairn Gorm and Ben Macdhui to Derry Lodge and returning the following day by way of Carn Ban Mor and Sgoran Dubh. In addition one or two parties were out on ski on the Drumochter hills and happened to meet there several members of the Ski Club of Great

*S.M.C.J. Vol. 21, No. 126, p. 380.
†S.M.C.J. Vol. 10, No. 60, p. 289.
**ibid. p. 291.

Britain. The sport was certainly growing in popularity and by the outbreak of the First World War membership of the Scottish Ski Club had increased from the original 100 in 1907 to 228. In October 1917 the first recorded expedition on Meall a'Bhuiridh was carried out, by a party of the Ladies' Scottish Climbing Club led by Mrs Mabel Jeffrey.

On the whole, however, there was still no really impressive swing of the mountaineering fraternity towards ski-ing. In the years between the wars a number of accomplished climbers did indeed discover that the two sports were not necessarily rivals, but could be complementary in providing the maximum amount of winter enjoyment. But the attitude generally was not that of today; it was still the exception rather than the rule for ski-ing in Scotland to be regarded as a highly skilled branch of mountaineering in its own right and not as an almost inferior way of passing the time.

The first centre in Scotland to achieve real popularity was the Ben Lawers area. Various factors combined to bring this about: the easy access from the hill-road which climbs above Loch Tay to Lochan na Lairige, then drops again to Glen Lyon; the open, grassy slopes on the flanking horseshoe of Meall Corranaich and Beinn Ghlas, and the fact that being situated so far from the sea, the hills hold the snow remarkably well. The hut which was erected by the Scottish Ski Club high in Coire Odhar could be a busy place indeed most fine week-ends in early spring.

These advantages still hold good, of course. The pleasant, south-facing running in Coire Odhar, catching all the sunshine that is going, is still immensely popular. With no tows there, a deal more effort in uplift may be needed, but the slopes are kinder to the tyro than those of Meall a' Bhuiridh and they are much more quickly reached from Glasgow or Edinburgh than the thronged snow-bowls of Cairn Gorm.

Ideas nevertheless are constantly changing, and after the end of the Second World War downhill only enthusiasts were being attracted more and more strongly by the possibilities of permanently installed mechanical aids. In addition, discerning members of the Scottish Ski Club were coming to appreciate more and more the advantages of another hill away from Ben Lawers altogether — Meall a'Bhuiridh. Rising from the edge of Rannoch Moor beside the eastern approaches to Glencoe, its north-facing slopes were found to have excellent snow-holding properties and in addition to offer running of a consistently high standard. Eventually, in 1951, Meall a'Bhuiridh came under serious scrutiny in the search for a 'playground' suitable for mechanisation. Observations were made over the following four winters and the best natural line was chosen and surveyed, with the result that the snow-cover was voted sufficiently reliable for both quantity and quality; a further recommendation was that the slopes were easily accessible from a main road rarely blocked by snow. In 1955 a ski-tow was erected on the top 900 feet of the mountain; in 1959 Scotland's first commercial winter sports company, White Corries Ltd, was formed; the following year the first chairlift was put up, obviating the wearisome plod up the lower slopes, and in 1963 a second tow was installed.

Above the top of the chairlift, at 2,090 feet, extensive plateau slopes open out and provide a variety of nursery runs. It is, however, higher still that the best of Meall a'Bhuiridh is to be found: runs of a high — some of a very high — standard, although still with a few not over-severe for the moderate performer. Names like Flypaper, Spring Run, Rannoch Glade, Massacre and West End are well-known and commanding of considerable respect. All start from the top of the tow system, with variants providing an enjoyable diversity. The minimum 'straight' descent is reckoned to be approximately 1,400 yards, with possible extension to about a mile and usually a gentle run-out available to the top of the chairlift. When really good conditions at the height of the season make it possible to ski right down to the foot of the chairlift, enthusiasts can enjoy one of the longest and best ski-runs in Scotland, measuring two miles and with a descent of 2,400 feet.

The lift system on Meall a'Bhuiridh can play a useful part in various expeditions southwards into the heart of the Black Mount range. For the most part these are long and demanding of a sound knowledge of mountaincraft: for example, some intricate direction-finding may be involved in poor weather and some of the south-facing slopes are avalanche-prone. The rewards, however, can be great, especially on a day of unbroken sunshine and sharp visibility, with views into the depths of Coire Ba — surely one of the finest corries in all Scotland — and beyond, far out across the patchwork of Rannoch Moor.

Away towards the other side of the country, on Speyside, developments in the ski-ing world happen so quickly as to be altogether bewildering. Each year seems to outstrip the one before in its deluge of glossy propaganda attracting more and more thousands to the snows of Cairn Gorm. Conditioning to package holidays and international ski schools, to mechanisation everywhere and to the sophisticated glamour-dream of après ski, all seems strangely far removed from genuine initiative in the true spirit of the hills.

On Cairn Gorm itself, at the time of writing, there are two chairlift systems: from above the main car park one can soar in comfort to the Middle Station and well-known White Lady Shieling, and thence again to the Ptarmigan restaurant not far below the summit at a height of 3,656 feet. In Coire na Ciste the uplift is provided by two shorter lifts which have recently been installed. In addition, to give access to the starts of some fourteen different runs in the two principal corries, nine ski-tows are available.

South of the main range of the Cairngorms, the hills above Glen Shee offer some of the most rewarding ski-ing in Scotland. A measure of its popularity may be seen in the fact that the seemingly huge car parks at the summit of the Cairnwell road can on occasion be inadequate to meet the demands made on them. The chairlift which operates from the roadside to near the top of The Cairnwell itself, a vertical distance of some 800 feet, and the tows on Carn Aosda and across the main road on Meall Odhar all have a remarkably heavy work-load to cope with. Touring, too, from hereabouts can be immensely varied and enterprising, whether westwards from The Cairnwell to Carn Gheoidh, a fractionally higher 'Munro', or from Glas Maol on the other side of the pass, away over a succession of rolling tops to the plateau of the White Mounth and Lochnagar itself. Here surely, if anywhere in Scotland, is opportunity for high-level Langlauf at its exhilarating best.

These days, however many there may be who are slavishly

dedicated to the *pistes* of Cairn Gorm or Meall a'Bhuiridh or
Glen Shee, there are certainly more and more enthusiasts
enjoying the greater freedom of genuine ski-touring.
Sometimes the narratives of their exploits find their way into
print — usually the print of the various club journals. More
often they remain unrecorded. And this is well; for there is still
a great deal to be said for the pleasure of being able to go out
and imagine that one is making a new find, however humble it
may be. In any event so variable are the conditions of surfaces
and weather — not forgetting sodden snow, howling wind and
freezing mist — that no two expeditions are ever exactly alike;
the hills which were 'discovered' by a Raeburn or a Naismith
three-quarters of a century ago and which have been skied
over a hundred times since, have still something new to offer
every day of each succeeding season.

As examples of supreme enjoyment two recent descriptions
might be chosen. The first is of an ordinary day on an
ordinary hill, the humble Perthshire 'Munro', Ben Chonzie:

> Who, for instance, finding himself accidentally on the top of Ben
> Chonzie in the summer, amid harebells and bumblebees, could imagine
> the epic struggle J.R. and the writer had there one February? Merrily
> they struck up the snow by Invergeldie burn, into the mist and the N.W.
> wind. When the slope became too steep to point the skis uphill, even with
> the aid of skins, they sidestepped laboriously, peering about to detect
> some easing of the slope. It steepened, and the wind howled and rattled
> through six frozen skins. The writer, faced with some 1,200 feet of side-
> stepping and conveniently hidden from J.R. by the mist, thought to
> remove these excellent skis and proceed more easily on foot. He was
> interested to discover that vibrams were no more comforting on the now
> very icy snow than were steel-edged skis, and to carry two six-foot planks
> in such a hurricane either up or down such a slope by means of steps
> poked out with two ski-sticks held in one hand was not to be thought of.
> So he side-stepped up to the top and found a great plateau and a blazing
> sun. The run down on the south side was pure joy, skating on the level
> with the wind, tacking skilfully with outstretched anoraks in
> pterodactylic delight, and then a weaving down from snowfield to
> snowfield by short steep and narrow bits, a maze of exhilaration. Thus
> did a humble mound, bad-tempered in a N.W. wind, provide first-class
> enjoyment and a refreshing change from ascents of the head-down, feet-
> kick variety.*

*"Skis in Scottish Mountaineering", by Geoffrey J.F. Dutton, S.M.C.J.
Vol. 26, No. 148, p. 122.

The second description is of no ordinary 'day' — it began at 3 a.m. and ended some 24 hours later — when the writer soloed his way from east to west across the High Cairngorms, 'bagging' five of the six main summits starting with Ben Avon and ending with Cairn Toul, thirty-four miles on skis with 8,700 feet of climbing. The April weather was ideal, the snow a typically varied Scottish mixture. At the North Top of Beinn a' Bhuird "a fine view opened out to the west. The two-mile descent to the Yellow Moss was the best ski run of the day, with glistening hard-packed powder in every direction. I swooped leisurely from side to side all the way down Coire Ruaraidh, and finally far out on to the Moss in a last straight run." On Ben Macdhui "the plateau was a continuous sheet of silky smooth snow." Late in the afternoon:

> The steep climb up Braeriach on skins was easy, on snow so hard in the shade that the skis scarcely left a mark, and yet not so icy and steep that the skins didn't grip. An hour later I was at the top, looking down a Coire Bhrochain precipice heavily sheathed in ice and frost. A bitterly cold breeze was blowing but the few clouds in the sky were all vanishing rapidly. It was good to look away from the glaring snow and ice for a moment, down past the cone of Carn Eilrig to the warm reddish-brown moors of Strath Spey, the green fields of Tullochgrue and the houses at Coylum among the pines.*

A recently published pocket guide which covers the ski-ing possibilities of fifty-seven hills and hill-groups from Kirkcudbrightshire to the Cairngorms, is guaranteed to whet the appetites of expert and rabbit alike. This is *Scottish Mountains on Ski* by Dr Malcolm Slesser,† a model of conciseness and a store of really excellent advice. The descriptive details include the general character of the expeditions, the probable length of season, access by car or bus, and the essential heights and times. Even more important, the standard of difficulty of each route is given, thus supplementing the heavy stress already laid on safety in the introductory section of general advice. Unfortunately the publication of the guide was followed by rather poor Scottish seasons, so that it did not come into its own as fully as

---

*"Cairngorm Langlauf", by Adam Watson, S.M.C.J. Vol. 27, No. 154, p. 351.
†West Col Productions, Reading, 1970

it undoubtedly would have done otherwise, and the second volume which Dr Slesser had planned was postponed. It is to be hoped that this is something easily put to rights by the return of better snow-coverings on the ridges and in the corries, and consequently by another surge forwards in adventurous high-level touring.

A dozen or so years ago the subject was raised of *Une Haute Route Ecossaise* and discussion followed of the various permutations and combinations that this might involve. Working from east to west, it might begin perhaps with Mount Keen, most easterly of the 'Munros', and end with the descent of Ben Nevis to Fort William. The Cairngorms would certainly have to be fitted in; indeed they would most likely provide the finest section of the whole tour. Equally, however, there would have to be much skilful route-planning if long, tedious stretches of walking were to be avoided. Also open to argument is the number of days that would be needed. Unlimited leisure, of course, would solve all problems, but in default of this, no one seems to have cut the allowance to less than five days, and even that would mean dispensing with such an unnecessary luxury as a tent. But whatever the ideal answer, the marathon would undoubtedly be a wonderful experience in good early spring conditions and could well become a real Scottish classic — for the expert.

Whatever one's approach, therefore, whether as downhill only or as dyed-in-the-wool ski-mountaineer, the Scottish hills have still a boundless supply of great things to offer. A hard season can open up totally unsuspected pleasures, in Galloway maybe or even in such humble areas as the Glen Fruin hills or the Campsies. Imagination roams further, northwards possibly to a traverse of all nine 'Munros' of the Fannichs or exploration of some of the loneliest country in Scotland at the head of Glen Strathfarrar. Even in Lochaber on the giant flanks of the Aonachs and the Grey Corries, or in the immense hinterland of the Monadh Liath, there is surely enough and more than enough scope, irresistibly tempting, for all.

12
Post-War Pattern

So much — so very much — has happened in the Scottish
hills since the end of the Second World War that it is almost as
difficult to remember what things were like those three
decades ago as it is to conjure up a picture of the future
another three decades hence. Not only in the world of
mountaineering have the changes been devastating: ski-ing
has acquired an unguessed-at new dimension; forestry and
hydro-electricity have had full scope and altered for good or
for ill much of the face of the countryside; the pony-trekkers
are out and about; the surveyors have been busy; even the
television teams, every now and again, have been venturing to
new locations in unusually high places.

Neart nan Gleann, 'power of the glens', proclaims the Gaelic
motto of the North of Scotland Hydro-Electric Board. And the
heraldic escutcheon with it, granted by the Lord Lyon King-
at-Arms in 1944, incorporates a shield with flashes of
lightning, representing electricity, putting out the light of an
old-fashioned 'crusie' lamp; a fir tree, stags and water gushing
from a rock complete the Highland symbolism.

Although it was not until after the war that hydro-
electricity got fairly into its stride in Scotland, the first
developments in the Highlands — for the production of
aluminium — had been initiated many years earlier. As far
back as 1896 the Foyers scheme, harnessing the famous
waterfall on Loch Ness-side, had been brought into use by the
British Aluminium Company. Then in 1904, after a decade of
plans and preliminaries, Parliamentary sanction was obtained
for the construction of the Blackwater Reservoir and the
utilisation of its outflow at Kinlochleven, the great new
industrial centre at the head of Loch Leven; construction was
under way by the following year and, thanks in large measure
to the efforts of the 2,000-3,000 navvies, had been completed
by 1909. Another fifteen years later work began on the biggest
hydro-electric project that till then had been attempted in

Britain, the Lochaber scheme involving fifteen miles of tunnel through Ben Nevis, from Loch Treig to Fort William.

Between 1930 and 1932 part of the upper catchment area of the River Tummel was developed for hydro-electric purposes by the Grampian Electricity Supply Company and two public supply stations were built, Rannoch operating on the impounded waters of Loch Ericht and Tummel Bridge on the waters of Loch Rannoch; interestingly enough, this supply is now re-used at the Clunie and Pitlochry stations as part of the much more recent and more extensive Tummel Valley scheme. The North of Scotland Hydro-Electric Board was formed in 1943 — taking over the Grampian Electricity Supply Company's projects in 1947 — and by the end of 1948 construction had well and truly started, with no less than twelve large hydro-electric schemes under way. The Board's first major project, Loch Sloy, had in fact been promoted in 1945 and started the following year, primarily to provide electricity for the industrial belt of Clydeside and Central Scotland. From the loch, which was lengthened and deepened, a two-mile tunnel led through Ben Vorlich, the now familiar four green pipelines dropping from its mouth to the power station on the shore of Loch Lomond. In the years which followed, an impressive number of projects, small as well as large, were brought to completion: Breadalbane, Tummel Valley, Garry-Moriston, Affric-Farrar-Beauly, Conon Valley, Loch Shin — the names are familiar enough, as indeed are those of such lesser schemes as Lussa or Loch Gair, Mucomir or Storr Lochs, in Skye. More recently the Cruachan section of the Awe scheme has attracted world-wide interest as the first large-scale pumped storage hydro-electric development in Scotland. Inaugurated by Her Majesty the Queen on 15th October 1965, the project on Ben Cruachan includes a massive-buttress type dam, its crest 1,315 feet above sea-level, built across the Allt Cruachan to form a high-level storage reservoir, and also a gigantic subterranean machine-hall housing the four combined pump-turbine units. Small wonder that the whole scheme has become a major tourist attraction of Argyll.

Just how much the work of the Hydro Board has contributed to or detracted from the mountain scene is a highly controversial point. Some of the power stations faced with the beautiful pink stone from Tarradale near Muir of Ord obviously enhance the views, while some of the dams in themselves are striking showpieces. The effects on the appearance of the lochs are not necessarily so praiseworthy. For example, the level of Loch Benevean, tucked away in its beautifully wooded gorge, is not allowed to vary greatly, and provision is made to maintain a minimum flow in the River Affric; but little is ever said about the 'tide-marks' round the shore of Loch Mullardoch, caused by the necessity to feed Loch Benevean. Perhaps, all things considered, an essential job has been done as well as it could have been.

Expressive in its own individualistic way of the new, post-war approach to the hills has been the extraordinary growth of interest in pony-trekking. So remarkable indeed has been its continuing popularity that in April 1973 there was even an anniversary celebration — a dinner and special trekking parade — at Newtonmore where it had all begun twenty-one years before.

In the old days, of course, hill ponies were much used — it is not easy to decide just how much — although as a means to an end rather than as a pleasurable pastime in itself.

One cross-country military campaign to overawe the clans, carried out in 1654 by Cromwell's General Monck, certainly sounds as though it was anything but fun. Monck commanded a force of horse and foot which included his own regiment, now the Coldstream Guards, and at one stage of the operation he found himself and his troops in the wilds of Ross-shire, near the head of Loch Monar, in some of the loneliest, most remote country in Britain. His own words are suitably graphic:

> 29th July — I came to Glenteuch in the Shields of Kintail, the night was very tempestuous and blew down most of the tents. In all this march we saw only two women of the inhabitants and one man. The 30th — The Army march't from Glenteuch to Brouling [in Glen Strathfarrar]. The way for neere five miles soe boggie that about 100 baggage horses were left behinde and many other horses bogg'd or tir'd. Never any horse men (much less an armie) were observed to march that way.*

*Transactions of the Gaelic Society of Inverness, Vol. 18, p. 70 and following. Quoted in S.M.C.J., Vol. 22, No. 132, p. 335.

Just over a century later, in 1769, Thomas Pennant rode through Glen Tilt from Blair Atholl to Braemar and found the track "the most dangerous and the most horrible I ever travelled: a narrow path, so rugged, that our horses often were obliged to cross their legs in order to pick a secure place for their feet." Queen Victoria, taking the same route another seventy-five years on, travelled by carriage as far as Forest Lodge, then on pony-back through to Bynack Shieling — actually less than ten miles and not really as impressive as some of her mountain expeditions. It is satisfying all the same recently to have found the ponies of Glen Tilt being used to follow the Queen's good example — animals belonging to the famous stud owned by the Duke of Atholl and trekking in summer through such pleasantly quiet and little known side-glens as Glen Diridh, Glen Mhaire and Glen Fender.

Early last century it seems to have been quite normal to climb Cairn Gorm and Ben Lawers on pony-back, and not so long afterwards a writer makes mention of opportunities on Ben Lomond:

> I believe there is a path by which ponies can reach the very top; and a good many of these useful animals are usually kept at the Rowardennan Hotel for the accommodation of stout, short-winded folks, who would not venture on such an arduous undertaking on 'shanks-naigie'.*

On Ben Nevis riding to the summit was recognised as quite the done thing up until the closure of the hotel at the end of the First World War. An old guide-book of 1916 gives the charge for a pony and guide as twenty-one shillings.

Newtonmore, where trekking as it is known today was first introduced, could hardly be better placed, with Glen Banchor and the Monadh Liath on the one hand and the glens of the Western Cairngorms not so very much further away on the other. Quite early on a special annual event to be arranged was a trek across the hills in September to the Royal Braemar games. Certainly if one should happen to meet a party of riders, perhaps idling round some corrie-rim high above Glen Feshie, the pastime up in Badenoch at least looks to be one well worth pursuing. No time was lost in following the

*A Tour through the Highlands of Perthshire, by Malcolm Ferguson (1870).

example set at Newtonmore, other centres being opened under the sponsorship of the Scottish Council of Physical Recreation (now the Scottish Sports Council), that at the Covenanters' Inn, Aberfoyle, soon becoming the largest in Britain. Today it is all taken entirely for granted; centres from the Solway to Sutherland and from Angus to the Western Isles offer opportunities that are literally endless for getting to know the hills and glens.

It would hardly be right, in tracing the post-war pattern of the story, to omit any reference to the increasing numbers of those who find that their interest in natural history is taking them more and more to the hills. One thinks, for example, of the botanists who delight in the alpine rarities to be found on the slopes of the Lawers group, high on the plateaux of the Cairngorms, or possibly in Angus beside the head-streams of the Isla in the lonely recesses of Canness Glen or in neighbouring Caenlochan.

For the ornithologists life has been made far too easy with the uplift on Cairn Gorm cutting out the hard work that used to be needed in the old days on the approach march to the high tops. The ptarmigan do not seem to be unduly concerned at the growing intrusion and any snow buntings which may be about can be sure to keep well out of harm's way. It is easier to feel sorry for *amadan mointeach*, the colourful, confiding 'foolish fellow of the peat mosses', the dotterel. Already there is evidence of unwarranted disturbance, and over-much interest, however well intentioned, can do great harm. It is reassuring that the dotterel, like the golden eagle, has enough good sense to have other haunts on the hills well away from the crowds.

Just as it is obviously to youngsters that pony-trekking appeals most strongly, so too have hill-walking and climbing come to be taken more and more for granted as activities attractive to the lower age groups.

Although it was back in 1948 that the Scottish Centre of Outdoor Training (as it was then called) came into being at Glenmore Lodge, the first seeds had in fact been sown much earlier than that, in 1938 and 1939, when pilot schemes were tried out at Guisachan in Glen Affric and at Gordon Castle in Morayshire. The warden in charge of these ventures was the late Lord David Douglas-Hamilton and his ideas were put

The summit rocks of
Braeriach, second
highest of the
Cairngorms

On the first ascent of
Chancellor Gully,
Am Bodach, Glencoe,
July 1949

Avalanche debris (March) in Coire nam Beith, Glencoe

Pony-trekking centre in the Castle grounds, Blair Atholl

further into practice just after the war by his brother, the late Lord Malcolm Douglas-Hamilton. As Air Training Corps Commandant for Scotland, the latter organised map-reading and hill-walking courses at Glenmore for groups of cadets, and so successful were these that it was an easy matter to persuade the Scottish Education Department to arrange for a lease of the lodge so that experimental outdoor courses for youngsters could be run. The first series duly began on 31st July 1948, the centre — the first civilian mountain training school in Britain — having an official opening by the Secretary of State for Scotland just over a month later.

Since those early days Glenmore has developed and prospered mightily. Today's training, based on the 'new' lodge (now almost twenty years old), has a more than ordinarily impressive look. Inevitably in winter and spring a heavy emphasis falls on ski-ing; in summer sailing and white-water canoeing provide tempting rival attractions. But the basic skills of mountaineering in all its aspects, summer and winter, are always at the heart of the syllabus. Mountain rescue and survival courses are run several times a year, while a significant introduction in recent years has been training and assessment for the Mountain Leadership and the further Mountaineering Instructors' Certificates. Lord Malcolm Douglas-Hamilton could hardly have guessed, even in those exciting experimental days of close on thirty years ago, just how astonishingly his vision would be fulfilled.

The high standards set at Glenmore are obviously invaluable, both so far as actual courses there are concerned and by way of comparison at centres elsewhere. The leadership certificates too, provided they are regarded in sensible perspective, serve what has now become an essential purpose. Unfortunately all too many mishaps in recent years have shown up the tragic consequences of ignorance and stupidity and downright carelessness; only too often the competence of leaders — glibly referred to as 'experienced mountaineers' — has been called in question. One has only to think for a moment of the fantastic number of young people out on the hills over any given week-end to appreciate the clamant necessity for adequate safeguards. Schools and colleges, scout troops, Duke of Edinburgh's Award schemes, adventure centres, local mountaineering clubs, 'action holiday' ventures — all, and more, have almost suddenly created a demand for sound, sensible leadership which can never be altogether adequately met.

Inevitably over the years since the war the toll of accidents has been tragically heavy. The list prepared annually from the reports of the Mountain Rescue Committee of Scotland seems never to grow shorter or to tell a less distressing story. Details are always illuminating; often they are quite incredibly disturbing. For example, it is interesting to note where precisely mishaps have occurred, how many of the casualties have been unacquainted with Scottish weather conditions, the ratio of climbers to hill-walkers and so on; it is downright sad to learn how many incompetents there are still who imagine that Wellington boots or high-heeled shoes are reasonable footwear for the hill, or that a map and compass are unnecessary luxuries. Ben Nevis, after all, has accounted for more climbers' deaths than the North Face of the Eiger and it is by no means always the year's blackest area.

It is hardly fair to compare too closely present day figures with those of the past. And yet it is difficult not to wonder why in 1970, 1971 and 1972 on the Scottish hills there were altogether fifty-six fatalities, of whom it could be said that half were genuine climbers, when in the first forty-one years of the Scottish Mountaineering Club's existence — until Norman Mowbray lost his life on the Crowberry Ridge in 1930 — there was not one single fatal accident to any member of the club.

Actual rescue techniques and call-out procedures have probably advanced more remarkably than any other branch of mountaineering. Time was when the most comfortable stretcher that could be expected after a mishap on Ben Nevis was one of the window-shutters of the Charles Inglis Clark hut. Nor are the days so very far distant when rescue teams had not even enough money to pay for spare torch batteries. Even just after the last war mountain rescue was only starting to become organised, depending entirely on the local police and shepherds, helped out by volunteers from the various clubs who had expressed willingness to be considered on call for certain specified areas. The R.A.F. mountain rescue service had come into being in North Wales midway through the war, primarily to go to the help of occupants of crashed aircraft. The first actual call-out was in July 1943 and by the end of that year official status had been granted. Then the following summer for the first time help was given to a civilian climber and thereafter it was recognised that being used in this way could be a valuable aid to training and in addition, of course, a most worth-while public service. In Scotland the R.A.F. teams at Kinloss and Leuchars gradually came to be called upon more and more often until their assistance was taken very much for granted. With the police and countless volunteers, they have certainly done work which is beyond praise.

In Glencoe, where so many of the roughest and technically most difficult rescues have had to be carried out, the local team under the leadership of Mr Hamish MacInnes and in harmonious collaboration with the police has done heroic work for many years now. Besides being a mountaineer with a world reputation, MacInnes is internationally known as an authority on rescue techniques, and some of the methods he has introduced have been widely adopted. One variation which inevitably has caught the public fancy has been his experimental training and actual use of avalanche-dogs, resulting in 1965 in the formation of the Search and Rescue Dogs Association. It is amusing to think of the crude methods of yesterday compared to all the sophistication of today, with easy radio communication, cableways and evacuation capsules, and, always in the background, the ready help of helicopters. There are in fact those who are of the opinion that the pendulum has swung too far the other way and that rescue call-outs nowadays happen all too easily and not always for truly valid reasons.

It would, however, be utterly wrong if the dark side were to be stressed so heavily as to obscure in any way the other, positive and bright side of the picture. For the fact is that there have been developments so swift, so radical, so far-reaching that the whole immensity of change could fairly be described as an explosion. New equipment and new techniques; new clubs, new climbing areas and new routes in an absolute deluge; almost unbelievably higher standards; enterprise at

home matched by internationally recognised enterprise
abroad; mechanisation and professionalism and changed
values — a transformation which, by and large, is enough to
make the mind reel.

   In Skye, not surprisingly, the areas hallowed by long
tradition have become still more popular and crowded. Yet
somehow an endless number of new lines — many of them
genuine rock-climbing masterpieces — manage summer after
summer to be squeezed in alongside the old familiar routes, so
that the diagrams in the guide-books must look to the
uninitiated a bewilderment of dots and lettering completely
impossible to decipher. Probably, however, the most
remarkable developments are two which have occurred away
from the nail-polished trade-routes altogether. The first of
these was on the 'wrong' side of the Ridge, the side
overlooking the immense lonely basin hidden away at the
head of Loch Coruisk. Here the faces of the Coireachan
Ruadha, or 'red corries' — so called from the outcrops of red
peridotite which occur in many places — have since 1950 been
found to offer climbing of the very highest order. A single gully
climb and a face route a short distance further along on Sgurr
Dearg were all that had been done previously, and that was
back in 1912; since then the crags had been completely
neglected. Now, considering the popular appeal of Skye rocks
ever since last century, it is almost unbelievable that a face
could have been discovered to merit the guide-book
description of 'the most impressive cliff in the Cuillin'. Yet
that is what in fact the 700-foot high section of the Coireachan
Ruadha on the sunless side of Sgurr Mhic Coinnich has
earned, with half a dozen top-grade mountaineering
routes — the classic King Cobra among them — to make the
commendation. The other particularly notable new area — as
sadly neglected in the past as the Coireachan Ruadha — is the
east face of the outlier, Blaven. Here in 1967, 1968 and 1969 a
sudden burst of activity produced a whole new selection of fine
routes, typical of the exacting and exposed climbing of today,
high above the screes of Central Coire.

   South into the sun from Skye, across the Cuillin Sound, the
hills of Rum have come more significantly into their own.
Rum has always been a particularly attractive island, partly
because its privacy was so jealously guarded in the old days

and forbidden fruits taste so much sweeter, partly because the rock-climbing there, while still hard enough for those who wish it, is more carefree than that on the Skye Ridge. Rum is now, of course, a national nature reserve under the jurisdiction of the Nature Conservancy, and permission is required for visiting parts of the island away from the Loch Scresort area. No doubt the fact that there is such a vast amount of interest ornithological, geological and botanical keeps even the most dyed-in-the-wool rock gymnast from taking his efforts there with too oppressive a seriousness.

Back on the mainland there has been a similar story. Climbing standards have been pushed up and up to such fantastic heights that the old ideas have been turned topsy-turvy and even the most ferocious-looking cliff-faces have lost their aura of impregnability. It would be impossible here — and intolerably tedious — to list the scores of new climbs that have been made in Glencoe, on Ben Nevis and in the North-West; there have, in fact, been so many recently that they have reached deluge proportions. Finding vaguely sensible names for them all has become something of a problem in itself and there has even been a certain amount of argument against recording new routes at all in the areas west of the Great Glen, where so much of the enjoyment obviously derives from the sense of discovery.

On Buachaille Etive Mor several excellent additions were made to the maze of popular routes on the Rannoch Wall, while another face further round, on the flank of the North Buttress and picturesquely named Slime Wall, also came under vigorous — and highly successful — attack. Down the glen the pioneers were equally enterprising, especially on Aonach Dubh, out-thrust black spur of Bidean nam Bian. On Aonach Dubh's west face, where at the start of the century George Abraham and his wife had contributed to the earliest chapter of the Glencoe story, the dramatic rock-curtain of E Buttress has given some of the finest climbing in the area. Three outstanding achievements on it date from 1958, 1959 and 1961 — Trapeze, Hee-Haw and The Big Top, all rated 'very severe' and varying in length between 400 and 520 feet. It was the last two of these routes which were chosen for the live TV show of rock-climbing in Glencoe, and they certainly provided some highly sensational viewing.

On Ben Nevis, as might be expected, the remarkable advance in standards has been reflected no less spectacularly than elsewhere. In summer the emphasis has tended to swing to the formidable frontage of Carn Dearg, north-west shoulder of the Ben. Here on the Great Buttress are some of the finest climbs in Scotland with an average length of only a little less than 1,000 feet. Route 1 was done as far back as 1931, but the real classics like Centurion, The Bat and Sassenach all belong to the fifties.

Across the country from Lochaber, both Lochnagar and its near neighbour Broad Cairn have been opened up in as spectacular a fashion as Ben Nevis, to a great extent by the very enterprising Aberdeen 'school'. Across the Dee valley, too, on the main massif of the Cairngorms some extraordinary 'discoveries' have been made since the war. For example, the magnificent Coire Sputan Dearg of Ben Macdhui, quite unaccountably receiving not a shred of interest in the past, suddenly began attracting attention in 1948, since when it has developed into the most popular corrie in the Cairngorms, with the exception of Lochnagar. The following year it was the turn of another corner of Ben Macdhui, Creagan a' Choire Etchachan, first explored by a Cambridge University party and yielding in subsequent years a whole series of climbs averaging some 400 feet in length. Finally attention turned to the 800-foot crag of Cairn Etchachan, where one of the first ascents, named Scorpion and one of the longest climbs in the Cairngorms, was actually made in December, giving a tough snow and ice contest lasting seven hours.

Quite apart from the traditional climbing grounds, new areas in an altogether bewildering profusion have been discovered, explored and then in due course meticulously noted. Some of these discoveries had been crags on familiar hills, ignored only because they were at comparatively low levels; others have been faces remarkably well endowed with good things but spurned because they were not on the flanks of 'Munros'; others again have been far removed from the hills altogether and seemingly quite humble. Many of these playgrounds taken in isolation would be of no particular significance, but considered as a whole they add a completely new dimension to the overall pattern up and down the country.

Two interesting new 'finds' in Inverness-shire only some twenty miles apart were Binnein Shuas, near the western end of Loch Laggan, and Creag Dubh, just west of Newtonmore overlooking the main road to Spean Bridge. The former crag was first explored in 1964, the latter in 1959; both have grown quite spectacularly in popularity. Perhaps this is hardly surprising so far as Creag Dubh is concerned, for its three rock-faces are all within ten minutes of the road and, facing south, are frequently warm and dry when crags at higher altitudes are anything but hospitable.

Yet more important still in the mountaineering story has been the opening up of another entirely new area — on Beinn Trilleachan, a hill of a modest 2,752 feet which looks across the head of Loch Etive and up Glen Etive to the two Buachailles linked by the deep parabola of the Lairig Gartain. A gleaming shield of granite slabs, not far up the hillside, but set at a high angle, had attracted an occasional speculative glance, but it was not until the summer of 1954 that the first route, named Sickle, was pioneered. Thereafter the tough armour, set with boss and overlap, attracted assault after assault so that in only nineteen years the total number of routes had been pushed up to thirty-one. Here was slab climbing at its finest — long, sustained and exposed — exactly after the hearts of the modernists.

In the old days minor 'back door' practice grounds were surprisingly few and far between. Glasgow enthusiasts scrabbled of a summer evening — as they still do — on the brittle bulges of the Whangie. In Edinburgh the faithful have always been more fortunate, with the many delectable — and illegal — problems of the Salisbury Crags to tempt them out at crack of dawn before officialdom in its wisdom feels obliged to turn other than a blind eye. Nowadays the picture is far different. The west can boast quite a range of novelties from the doubtfully sublime on Dumbarton Rock — claimed to be superior to the Whangie — to the patently ridiculous of the Old Kilpatrick Rubbish Shoot, on which the most sensational move appears to be using the branch of a big tree "to catapult you up unclimbable rock, to land on a roll of barbed wire."*
The east nevertheless still clearly has the best of the bargain,

*S.M.C.J. Vol. XXX, No. 164, p. 184.

with Traprain Law near Haddington, with some seventy routes up to 100 feet in length, also the strenuous Railway Wa's at Currie, described as "the best finger-training grounds around Edinburgh" and where the principal hazard appears to be the high incidence of stonefalls "befor the local urchins' bedtimes."* In the far north, with long, worthwhile routes still discoverable high up, fewer such minor crags, real or artificial, attract attention; in the south inevitably there is more clutching at straws and one can even sink so low as to trespass across the Border to sample some gymnastic delights on anglicised Cheviot outcrops.

Symptomatic of all this phenomenal upsurge of activity and rise in climbing standards has been the increased share in top-class international mountaineering by Scots who have acquired their skills on the home hills. To some extent this is highlighted by the comparatively poor record of earlier years. Admittedly Professor Norman Collie had accomplished great things on the rock peaks of the Lofoten Islands and in the Alps and had shared with Mummery and Hastings in the assault on Nanga Parbat. Harold Raeburn, who died in 1926, had a brilliant record of climbs abroad: the Dolomites, Norway, the Alps — where he made the first British guideless ascents of the Zmutt Ridge of the Matterhorn and the Viereselgrat of the Dent Blanche — two visits to the Caucasus, Kangchenjunga and finally the 1921 Everest expedition. So, too, had W.N. Ling, to whom Raeburn dedicated his book, *Mountaineering Art*, and who partnered the latter on all his most daring climbs in Norway, the Alps and the Caucasus. By and large, however, outstanding Scottish achievements were few and far between.

With the Second World War ideas changed. No longer did the old vast-scale expeditions, outrageously costly and involving armies of porters, seem quite so necessary or have the same appeal. The pendulum had begun to swing; indeed it was to swing far the other way, with the mounting of small uncomplicated enterprises, many of them carried out on shoestrings — and mighty short shoestrings at that.

---

*The Railway Wa's, Currie, by D. Haston (Climbers' Guide to Creag Dubh and the Eastern Outcrops, G. Tiso, Edinburgh, 1967.)

Two four-man Scottish expeditions — to the Garhwal Himalaya in 1950 and to the country between Katmandu and Everest in 1952 — showed something of what could be done. In the autumn of the intervening year W.H. Murray had been deputy leader of Eric Shipton's Everest reconnaissance party; Tom MacKinnon was a member of the successful expedition to Kangchenjunga in 1955. The only disappointment — and that a big one — was that no Scot was invited to go to Everest in the great year, 1953.

Many books could be written — some indeed have been — about the exploits abroad over the next two decades. Some of the achievements — as, for example, the first ascents of the Mustagh Tower and of Rakaposhi in the Karakoram, success shared with the Russians on Pik Kommunizma in the Pamirs, the long-drawn-out ordeal of the Eiger Direct, Camp 6 on the south-west face of Everest — have placed Scottish mountaineers on an equal footing with the best in the world. North face *tours de force* in the Alps are taken nowadays very much for granted; the Andes and Antarctica, the Atlas Mountains and the rock walls of Yosemite have all become familiar; and members of the Ladies' Scottish Climbing Club have had their notable share too, by mounting the first expeditions composed entirely of women ever to explore and climb in the high Himalaya and, later, in the Staunings Alps of Greenland.

One man who played a particularly inspiring part in many of these achievements abroad was Dr Tom Patey. Long before his death in May 1970 while roping down from the top of The Maiden on the north coast of Sutherland, Patey's prowess had become legendary, the fantastic list of his achievements having included many dazzling successes overseas from the Alps and Norway to the Himalayas. By a tragic coincidence two other outstanding mountaineers also lost their lives in 1970: Ian Clough, who had climbed five of the six North Faces in the Alps and had done great things in South America, was killed by a falling serac on Annapurna, and Jim McArtney, described by Patey as "the most accomplished winter mountaineer of his generation", was overwhelmed by a slab avalanche on Tower Ridge, Ben Nevis, along with two companions. Only eight years previously an accident during the Russo-British expedition to the Pamirs had robbed Scottish mountaineering of Robin Smith, just twenty-three years old, yet already with a record of some of the hardest, most brilliantly conceived routes ever attempted in this country. It was a particularly heavy toll that had been exacted in so short a span of years.

The full story of Tom Patey's achievements could cram many volumes. His medical practice for the last nine years of his life was in Ullapool, yet so enterprising was his climbing that there was hardly a single area in the length and breadth of Scotland which did not receive the imprint of his brilliance. He served his apprenticeship in rock-work on the cliffs of the Buchan coast, then put his skill and daring to excellent use on the granite of the Cairngorms, starting in 1951 the audacious pioneering which over the years was to earn him his immense reputation. With an uncanny ability to size up the possibilities of a rock-face, he set an almost incredible pace as an innovator, whether it was in Wester Ross or Sutherland or Skye, with a classic like Vertigo Wall on Creag an Dubh Loch, "one of the hardest climbs in the Cairngorms", or exploration of some obscure, barely noticed face such as the Glenbeg Crags near Strathvaich Lodge, or a minor outcrop like Strone Nea overlooking the Braemore-Ullapool road near the head of Loch Broom. All was grist for his insatiable, intriguing mill.

In other ways too Tom Patey was unique: a first-rate musician with a devastating sense of humour, he poked fun mercilessly in verse and song at all and sundry — not omitting himself — and his tireless merrymaking will long be remembered by the many who knew and climbed with him. Some of the articles describing his expeditions, contributed mainly to the various club journals, are among the most amusing ever written and, unlike so many of their kind, bear any amount of re-reading. No reputation was safe from the shafts of his pungent wit, yet there was nothing vindictive about his satire, which, unlike that used by some of his more heavy-handed imitators, was intended to be hilarious, not cruel.

It is, of course, altogether disproportionate to write of Tom Patey thus at such length when there are after all so many other Scots of his era with brilliant mountaineering records both at home and abroad to their credit. It would be invidious, however, to mention some of the latter and not others, especially perhaps as most are still making history with their exploits. Surely rather it may be allowed for Patey, for all his unorthodoxy and uniqueness, to be taken as symbolising the spirit of the last two decades — the enthusiasm, the enterprise, the skill, the daring. I hope this will not be grudged and that into these sketchy notes on his achievements will be read something of the modern attitude generally to the wealth of good things our hills have continued to offer in recent years.

Probably it was on the advancement of winter mountaineering that Patey made his greatest impact — all the more remarkable as it was at a time when standards on snow and ice, aided by imaginative new techniques, were being pushed up to limits seemingly on the very verge of the impossible. If, for example, one leafs through the guide-book to the Lochnagar area,* one is struck immediately by the number of times Patey's name occurs in the records of first ascents; look more closely and there is no mistaking the quality of those winter classics of the fifties — Tough-Brown Traverse, "One of the finest climbs on the mountain"; Parallel Buttress, "For long one of the major winter problems"; Eagle Ridge Direct, "Under genuine snow and ice conditions, the hardest of the Lochnagar climbs", and so on. On Ben Nevis he shared in the epic success of Zero Gully, notable for the excessive steepness and technical problems of its first 400 feet and eyed many times previously as a glittering prize to be won. In the north-west he found almost unlimited scope for breaking new ground everywhere in the magnificent country right, as it were, on his Ullapool doorstep.

One area which particularly attracted Patey — and indeed which draws many others of the present-day winter experts back and back again — is Coire Ardair of Creag Meaghaidh, the massive hill of many 'tops' which overlooks Loch Laggan. Patey came to know the corrie intimately from leading a number of fine snow and ice climbs, but undoubtedly his most remarkable exploit was a 'girdle traverse' right across the face one day in mid-February 1969. He started after midday on a

*Climbers' Guide to the Cairngorms Area, Vol. 2 (Scottish Mountaineering Trust).

venture which had once been reckoned to need two bivouacs en route. And he climbed the whole way solo.

> Once in a while (he observed in his subsequent classic account*) it is very refreshing to climb alone. The practice is traditionally indefensible. I will therefore attempt to defend it.
>
> There are two cardinal precepts in mountaineering: 1.) The leader must not fall. 2.) The leader must climb as if the rope was not there. The first commandment is self-evident. No useful purpose could be served by a leader falling except to provide his followers with belaying practice. For the second commandment, there is only one way to ensure that a leader climbs as if his rope was not there — take away the rope. Now, it is also a fact that two men climbing unroped are no more secure than one. *Ergo* — the best solution is to climb solo. Q.E.D.
>
> By tradition the climber who habitually climbs alone is regarded as reckless. Nothing is further from the truth, because if he were other than safe, he would be dead. The main attraction of solo climbing is the freedom of movement one enjoys. The sensation is akin to coasting down the motorway after being held up at every set of traffic lights in Glasgow. You keep in top gear and your performance improves correspondingly.

As he proceeded on his amazing 'crab-crawl' across the high-angled, snow-plastered face, he found he had struck top form.

> Whatever the source of my elation, it was certainly not my reserves of armoury, which consisted of two ice-screws and one diminutive ring-spike — no selection for a crisis. My boots, equally uninspiring, were making one of their final farewell appearances. As with ageing Prima Donnas, money — or the lack of it — was the reason for these repeated performances. Earlier in the day I had been able to waggle my big toe through a large hole in the leather. This had then seemed an amusing party trick but I had now lost the point of the joke and, for all I knew, the point of the toe as well.

In the end, thanks to his speed and superb skill, he finished the climb — which was to have needed two nights out — in exactly five hours.

For sheer enjoyment, however, it is probable that Patey put far before everything else the first winter traverse of the Cuillin Ridge, in 1965. The exhilaration of this long February expedition — two arduous days in superb conditions of weather, ice and snow — is communicated to the reader in bumper measure in the account he wrote afterwards. In parts the brand of humour is productive of the kind of uncontrolled

---

*S.M.C.J. Vol. XXIX, No. 161, p. 233. Also in *One Man's Mountains* (Gollancz, 1971), p. 124.

mirth which does the soul a power of good, yet never are the difficulties played down in such a way as to de-value the expedition in the slightest.

> One abseil remained. Then we coiled up the rope for the last time and each of us wandered silently and independently along the final mile of scree-speckled Ridge to Garsbheinn, the final outpost of the Ridge. Beyond lay the blue Atlantic, warm and inviting in the afternoon sun. Down there by the shore a different world awaited us — a world of colour and contrast. In one searing whooping glissade of 2000 feet we returned to it. It was indeed good to be back. Our two-day journey in the winter Cuillin and the twelve-hour 'tarantella on ice' when crampon tips and ice-axe spike were our only contacts with tangible reality, now all seemed a strange and wonderful fantasy.
>
> A little older in wisdom, a little younger in spirit, we marched back over the moors to Glenbrittle. Down there in Cuillin Cottage, Mrs Campbell would be waiting for us with supper. It was a long-standing invitation that we fully intended to keep . . .
>
> There are many ultimates in mountaineering and every generation finds its own Last Problem. The five others who shared the first winter traverse of the Cuillin Ridge probably feel the same way as I do. There are many harder and more exacting routes, and many more still to be explored, yet I feel confident that the Winter Traverse of the Main Ridge will always retain its place as the greatest single adventure in British Mountaineering.*

A notable breakaway from the habitual mountain playgrounds — made in part to escape from the more crowded ridges and faces, although more especially for its own sake — has been sea-cliff climbing. Developed and expanded very largely since the war, this new form of specialisation offers vast scope for originality and has already attracted quite a sizeable following. It is not, of course, by any means a Scottish prerogative; over the years there have been innumerable assaults on cliff-faces all round the coast of Britain, and much of its appeal today is obviously to those mountainless enthusiasts who have to live south of the Bristol Channel. In Cornwall especially, where the accompanying delights of surf and sunlight are to be experienced at their most lavish best, it has for long had its devotees; it was there during the war that the Marines were introduced to cliff-assault techniques prior to D-Day by Army commando

*S.M.C.J. Vol. XXVIII, No. 156, pp. 86-7. Also in *One Man's Mountains* (Gollancz, 1971), pp. 102-3.

instructors and there too afterwards, as in North Devon, that many National Servicemen on specialist training discovered the pleasures of pioneering bold new routes.

In Scotland the pre-war story was not particularly distinguished. A few scrambles and traverses on one or two of the Inner Hebrides; tentative exploration of the rocks at Fast Castle in Berwickshire; some short climbs on the buttresses and pinnacles of the Isle of May; a few more desultory exploits elsewhere round the coast — and not really very much besides. The one exception was probably round the big sea inlet of Longhaven, between Peterhead and Cruden Bay, where in the 1930s the enthusiasts of Aberdeen enjoyed the exposure of the rough red granite walls.

In the decades since the war the picture has changed out of all recognition. On the mainland from the Mull of Galloway to the immense sandstone wall of Clo Mhor near Cape Wrath, in the islands from Islay to the Orkneys, new challenges have been sought out, accepted and happily met. Areas previously unsuspected now claim pages of routes in the guide-books. And still exploration continues.

Most spectacular of all have been the climbs on the great surf-lashed sea-stacks which present such obviously sensational challenges off our coasts. Not in the least surprisingly it was once again Tom Patey who, more than anyone else, realised the unique climbing possibilities on Scotland's stacks, who brought his outstanding skill and audacity to bear on so many of the early assaults and who popularised them so brilliantly in his writing. It was not by chance that he was sometimes given the affectionate nickname of 'Dr Stack'. And it was much more than ordinarily tragic that it was on a sea-stack — the quartzite pillar named The Maiden, off Whiten Head in Sutherland — that he should have fallen to his death.

That brilliant outside programme, the televised climbing of the Old Man of Hoy in 1967, had millions of viewers literally clutching their armchairs. It showed without deceit the kind of rock problem that the most skilled of our modern cragsmen find particularly to their taste. But it may well have created the impression that the Old Man was an altogether isolated effort, a 'once only' spectacular singled out specially for the benefit of the BBC. This was certainly not so. On the contrary there have been many more stacks falling to equally determined assaults — pinnacles like the Great Stack of Handa or the Old Man of Stoer, Am Buachaille near Sandwood Bay in Sutherland, or further rock-towers in Orkney such as Standard Rock off Costa Head (involving a swim of seventy-five yards to its base), Stack o' Roo, or the crazy topheavy-looking Castle of Yesnaby.

Recently, too, and perhaps inevitably, thoughts have been turning to the toughest problems of all, on St Kilda. Already the highest of the cliffs there, the vertiginous 1,400-foot face of Conachair on the main island of Hirta, has had a reconnaissance to itself — a reconnaissance which was meant to occupy less than three days and which, because of mountainous seas, in fact occupied nearly three weeks. This is obviously the kind of hazard that must always be taken into consideration in making any sort of plans for St Kilda. As Martin Martin observed of the outlier Boreray nearly three centuries ago, "This isle is very high and all rock, being inaccessible except in a calm, and there is only one place for landing, looking to the south"; a verdict which has been confirmed more than once by those who have had first-hand experience of rocky landings there in recent years.

It is amusing to reflect that, with a return to those forbidding crags out in the Atlantic, scene of countless daring feats so many centuries ago, the wheel has now turned almost full circle.

13

The Heritage

In these days of couldn't-care-less pollution, of vandalism just for the fun of it, of accumulations of litter so unsightly as to be nauseating, it would be miraculous indeed if our hills were escaping unscathed. In fact, the winds may blow as fresh as ever they did across the high plateaux, the snows may fall as pure winter after winter, but we in our prodigality are making distressingly sure in many ways that the most glorious natural heritage in the world is put in very grave jeopardy.

It is disturbing to say the least to learn of no less than 370 sackfuls of litter being gathered on a Countryside Commission clean-up in the Cairngorms in the course of a single summer week-end, the 'finds' including approximately 5,000 tins. An operation worthy of the highest praise, but one which should hardly have been necessary.

In June 1971 a Scottish Mountaineering Club member particularly familiar with Glas Maol, the fine ski-mountain on the Perthshire-Angus-Aberdeenshire border above the old Devil's Elbow, was disgusted to find an outsize scattering of rubbish at the summit left by a service unit. Over 120 items of litter were counted.

This consisted of unused packets of toilet paper, packets of oatmeal, many tubes and tins of jam (some intact and some partially used), empty tins of soup, meat and jam, stale bread, metal tent pegs, some wooden fencing posts removed from the plateau fence, many used storage batteries, and numerous service telephone pads, some in code with the name and address of the unit. They had unsuccessfully tried to hide some of their rubbish by pushing articles between stones on the cairn or half burying them in shallow hollows nearby. Unfortunately, they had also pulled out many stones from the cairn itself, from the vegetation nearby and from a Land-Rover track on the way to Cairn of Claise, to make wind-shelters. No attempt had been made to demolish the wind-shelters or fill up the gaping holes in the vegetation and this added to the general untidiness.*

*S.M.C.J. Vol. XXX, No. 164, p. 187.

In the Applecross
hills: the buttresses
of Sgurr a'
Chaorachain
and A' Chioch

Entrance to the
National Trust for
Scotland's mountain
visitor centre on
Ben Lawers

The Old Man of Stoer, Sutherland, climbed for the first time
in June 1966

Fortunately the incident had a happy sequel, for the officer commanding the unit, on being given the details in no uncertain terms, brought swift retribution on the offenders and had the whole mountain-top put to rights inside a week. In addition he had his men out again shortly afterwards on a major clean-up of Glen Clova.

In the summer of 1970 landing at Village Bay, St Kilda, was marred by a hideous, jarring cacophony — bulldozers and dump-trucks, compressors and cement-mixers, all vying with each other in frenzied chorus; even the St Kilda wrens had difficulty in making themselves heard. Up at the wind-scoured summit of Oiseval, almost 1,000 feet above the bursting surf, there was still no escape. No doubt matters improved when the particular construction work then in progress for the Army came triumphantly to an end; perhaps, too, efforts were made to collect the litter, the rusting beer cans and the inevitable fluttering polythene; but for one visitor at least the unique sanctity of St Kilda had been irreparably destroyed.

In the old days 'gardyloo' was the familiar warning cry of housewives in Edinburgh before throwing their slops out of the window into the street. Appropriately enough 'Gardyloo' was the name given to the gully falling directly from the summit of Ben Nevis where the old observatory (later the hotel) was situated; it must have been a most convenient rubbish-chute, and down it too must have gone many of the bits and pieces of the hotel itself when eventually it was closed and left to disintegrate. One can hardly imagine the local Swiss *Kurverein* allowing some building at the summit of their highest mountain merely to rot and rust and decay into oblivion. The unfortunate fact is that, however good we may be at building, we are usually quite deplorable at tidying up. It is difficult to forget the ugly black weal that was cut deep across the moorland shoulder behind Rackwick Bay, when the ascent of the Old Man of Hoy, in Orkney, was televised in 1967. Not that this wanton scarring of our hillsides is in any way a new trait in our national make-up: one has only to lift one's eyes to the slopes of Meall Odhar above Tyndrum to see all too plain evidence of the mess that was made when the old lead mines were worked back in the eighteenth and the first half of the nineteenth century.

Turning again to the present it is right and proper that everything should be done to encourage our home-bred winter sports enthusiasts. The mass enjoyment of the ski-slopes of Cairn Gorm, the Glen Shee hills and Meall a'Bhuiridh is something which has come to stay. And inevitably, as part of this, mechanisation is indispensable; the chairlifts and the tows have for long enough now been taken very reasonably for granted. Too often, all the same, the other side of the picture is forgotten — or ignored: the debris and the scars that are left when the snows have melted. In the chapter which includes a description of the splendid ski-playground above the Cairnwell pass, in the S.M.C. district guide-book to the Cairngorms, there are some suitably pungent comments on this:

> These construction jobs have in places exposed mud, bare gravel and churned-up peat, due to caterpillar tractors carrying material. In these places there is more erosion, some impassable peat morasses have formed, and the immediate surroundings of the buildings are an eyesore covered with dirty gravel and bare of vegetation. More litter has appeared, ranging from the usual bottles and tins to pieces of snow-fencing, metal and wire parts from the tows, and in one case in 1966-67 to a complete, abandoned tractor. It is to be hoped that this damage can be covered up by plant life, and that the appearance of the place will not go on deteriorating until the tourists who are attracted are eventually repelled.
>
> The man seeking solitude or silence will therefore be advised to go elsewhere.*

It is comforting, of course, to reflect that so far the winter sports deluge has been contained within relatively narrow bounds. Nevertheless, there is no saying what tomorrow's 'developments' may bring forth — Ben Wyvis, for example, has already been given serious consideration; ominous mention has been made of the long northern slopes of Aonach Mor, in Lochaber, and Carn Ban Mor would be an obvious choice for mechanisation if ever the long-mooted road through Glen Feshie were to be constructed. It is just to be hoped that if these or other areas are taken over, the conservation lessons of the past will be borne very seriously in mind.

There is, regrettably, yet another, more insidious, way in

*Scottish Mountaineering Club District Guide, *The Cairngorms*. Fourth Edition, 1968 (West Col Productions, Reading).

which our heritage is being debased: by the attitude of so many present-day climbers, expressed both in their actual approach to the hills and in the descriptions which subsequently they choose to inflict on too long-suffering readers.

It is of course in the nature of things that one not so young should be critical of modernity; it is equally inevitable that such criticism will be ridiculed as old-fashioned, 'stuffed shirt', hardly worth half an ear. And yet, offered sincerely and in sorrow rather than in anger, it may nevertheless have in it something which is of value.

Mountaineering as a sport is presumably meant to be enjoyed, even if often enough — standing shivering perhaps at some wind-chilled belay with iced rain percolating down one's neck — there may be cause to wonder what indeed there is enjoyable about it. But it is surely permissible to ask if things have not got more than a little out of perspective. Certainly standards nowadays are so incredibly high, the razor-edge of risk has to be trodden with so delicate a balance, that to play the game of top-class mountaineering at all must inevitably demand a good deal of cynical levity. But even to this there must be limits. Does it really, one wonders, add to anyone's pleasure for life itself to be held quite so cheaply as it is in the idiom of today? Surely if life does not matter, then all the rest goes by the board. Gambling for the highest stakes, whether it be on Everest or the Chamonix aiguilles, on Ben Nevis ice or Arran granite, is not something that can be indulged in for self alone; always it must contain the risk of incalculable hurt to others. By all means let the standard of our Scottish climbing be pushed to the limit — if such indeed exists — but let it be remembered at the same time that if the ultimate sanction goes, the sport itself becomes meaningless.

Unfortunately in the writing which goes with such climbing, whether in books or in articles, quite literally anything goes nowadays. Foul language, irreverence, debunking, blasphemy; everything which increases a man's stature in his own eyes — if hardly in others' — is considered *à la mode*. This is, of course, a sign of the times quite apart from the hills altogether, and it is always the popular thing to do to run with the pack. But the old days when writing could be

inspiring and pleasurable, when humour was healthy and not
sick, seem largely to have vanished; under-playing everything
in the modern style has taken the place of the Victorian
propensity for over-playing and exaggeration; and the one can
be as boring as the other. Unfortunately Scotland has not
escaped. It is almost rare nowadays to happen on any
accounts of note other than those of top-grade climbs, almost
always studiously — and wearisomely — derisive. The old
idea that the Scottish hills had something very special to offer
by way of all-round rather than specialised enjoyment seems
hopelessly outmoded if not actually dead. And yet those who
were so foolish as to live in the days when there was no shame
in admitting that a well-known classic route could actually be
enjoyable, who were so ingenuous as to value something of
truth and sanctity, may at least be excused if they believe they
had the best of the deal and that the majority of climbers
today for all their tremendous achievements — and they
really are tremendous — have nevertheless lost something
immeasurably worth while.

Fortunately, over against so much that can give cause for
concern, there is the other side of the picture altogether. There
is any amount that is encouraging both in the recent past and
in the present, any amount to allow optimism to win the day.

It is well, for instance, to look back for a moment and recall
briefly the immense debt of gratitude that is owed to the late
Percy Unna. This very remarkable man, a former president of
the Scottish Mountaineering Club, died in 1950 with only a
few of his contemporaries aware of a fraction of what he had
done for the hills he loved. In 1935 and 1937, when the
Glencoe and Dalness estates came up for sale, it was very
largely thanks to his lead and also to his most generous gift,
made anonymously, that they were purchased and handed
over to the National Trust for Scotland. Later in 1937 he
entered into seven-year covenants which provided the Trust
with a fund of £20,500 known as the Mountainous Country
Fund, while at the same time a committee was appointed to
advise on further purchases. The first of these was the Forest
of Kintail, acquired in 1944 through another extraordinarily
generous — and anonymous — gift by Unna. In 1951,
through the Mountainous Country Fund, the Trust was able

to purchase Ben Lawers and adjacent summits to the extent of 8,000 acres. Finally, with further valuable bequests at the time of his death, the Unna funds rose in total to an approximate £300,000.

Unna himself, as well as being a keen mountaineer, was of a most original turn of mind. As a civil engineer he was noted for his inventive genius and this was called on when the equipment for the early Everest expeditions was being designed. In 1937, after Dalness Forest had been handed over to the National Trust for Scotland, he set out his views on the interpretation of the request which had been made that the Trust would "be asked to undertake that the land be maintained in its primitive condition for all time with unrestricted access to the public." One of these views, interestingly and wisely enough, was that "the hills should not be made easier or safer to climb."

It is hardly necessary to underline the benefit of the Unna bequests today — the safeguarding of Glencoe, so vulnerable to pressures of many kinds; the magnificent scenery of Kintail; Ben Lawers, with its wealth of Alpine flora and now — opened in June 1972 — the visitor centre which is playing an important educational role in caring for all that is best in Scotland's scenery.

Quite one of the most cheering enterprises of recent years has been the work of the Mountain Bothies Association. Having for its aim "To maintain simple unlocked shelters in remote country for the use of walkers, climbers and other outdoor enthusiasts who love the wild and lonely places", the Association has been particularly careful to avoid detailed publicity, so that its very real achievements are not as widely known and appreciated as they would otherwise have been.

It all started in 1965 when a small group of enthusiasts set to work renovating a derelict cottage at Tunskeen in the Galloway hills — an exercise which involved man-handling cement and corrugated iron sheeting over miles of moorland and even panning sand from a nearby stream. In the end the success of this project aroused so much enthusiasm that the idea of forming some kind of association was born and the M.B.A. duly came into being at Dalmellington, in Ayrshire. Those mainly responsible were — as one member graphically put it — "pass-storming cyclist types from Manchester", but wider support was quickly forthcoming and in less than a year the membership total had cleared the 200 mark. Those now involved include outdoor enthusiasts of all kinds — hill-walkers, rock-climbers, rough-stuff cyclists, potholers, naturalists and many engaged in education; in addition there are gamekeepers, wardens, foresters and a number of landowners. From the start the motivating idea has been, of course, to set about the voluntary and unobtrusive renewal of near-derelict mountain bothies which formerly had provided shelter for workers of different kinds in some of the most remote hill-country of Britain. It was estimated that there were literally hundreds of these bothies scattered throughout Scotland and England, and the long-term policy that was agreed was to make a survey of them and, where the owner's consent was obtained, to make them into suitable mountain shelters. Remarkable results have been achieved since the Association was formed. Some of the projects — for instance the renovation of the highly inaccessible Dibidil bothy on Rum — make stories of classic quality. In one year alone (1973) work went on in the Pennines and in Galloway, in the Cairngorms and Torridon, on Loch Lomondside and in Prince Charlie's country, often in co-operation with members of colleges and the various mountaineeering clubs.

What is unusually interesting about the Association is that the main benefits are those which derive from helping others, occasionally even from helping to save lives; members themselves do not have a great deal to show for their support other than hard work and even often enough the provision of financial assistance. There are no special privileges so far as bothy use is concerned, while an exemplary code has been drawn up to make it normal practice to leave every place visited cleaner, tidier and better stocked than it was previously. The whole endeavour is, in short, idealistic and unselfish, the very antithesis of that all too common vandalism which has left so many of these remote shelters fouled and pillaged and frequently in that ultimate state of tragedy — a scattering of charred ruins.

As one turns to the future and thinks of some of the ways in which the hills could be affected, it is essential — if not at all easy — to try to take a fairly balanced, reasonable view. There are, for example, excellent grounds for believing that Forestry Commission policy has won clear of most of the bad mistakes of the early days and is finding an acceptable middle way amid the rival claims of industrial needs, job creation and tourism; the forest parks have many very real attractions and hill-slope planting is no longer as deplorably unattractive and obstructive as it was formerly. Of hydro-electric work both the best and the worst results have been clear for years now for all to observe: admirable man-created lochs and tragically parched river-beds, power-stations of the most pleasing construction and yet 'tide-mark' scarring of loch shores irremediably offensive to the eye; schemes like Affric-Farrar-Beauly, Tummel Valley and Breadalbane successfully achieved and in operation, like Glen Nevis and Fada-Fionn, behind Loch Maree, never started and — it is fervently to be hoped — now sensibly forgotten. Some day, no doubt, the road from Deeside to Speyside by way of Glen Feshie will be built; first mooted more than two centuries ago as a useful through-link to Ruthven barracks, its value can be even more cogently argued today, however much one may object to such further intrusion on solitude. For the road across Rannoch Moor from Rannoch station to Kingshouse there is less excuse; indeed one can see no good reason for it at all and it too would be better forgotten.

The hills will remain. Their secrets, their beauty, their peace will continue to inspire and enchant in the ways that have been known and absorbed and valued all down the centuries. Clansman and shepherd, Redcoat and Covenanter, drover and tourist, general and prince, king and queen and crofter, artist and scientist and mountaineer have all shared in our heritage. Let those who come after never forget.

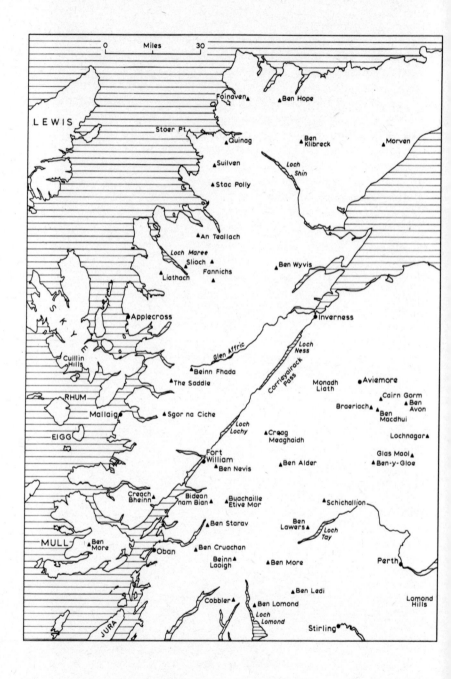

INDEX

A

Abraham, Ashley, 119, 121
Abraham, George, 119, 121, 165
Achintee, 86, 90, 135
Achnacarry, 142
Agag's Groove, 136
Ailsa Craig, 16, 68, 74
Airgiod Bheinn, 28
Allival, 19, 22
Allt a' Mhuilinn, 113, 127
Alpine Club, 83, 107, 112
Am Basteir, 26, 115
Am Bodach, 28
An Teallach, 28, 74, 118
Aonach Beag, 112
Aonach Dubh, 31, 121, 134, 165
Aonach Eagach, 15, 21, 57, 134
Aonach Mor, 60, 178
Applecross, 28, 46
Ardgour, 24, 56
Argyll's Eyeglass, 43
Arran, 14, 16, 28, 43, 44, 98, 99, 120, 145
Arrochar, 109, 130, 131
Askival, 19, 22
Aust, Hon. Mrs Murray, 71
Aviemore, 24, 145

B

Baddeley's Guide, 56, 107
Bailey, Rev. James, 70, 71
Baker, Ernest A., 118-21
Ballachulish, 21, 30, 136
Barlow, Dr Guy, 121, 125, 126
Barra, 22, 37
Bass Rock, 37
Bealach nam Bo, 46

Beinn Airidh Charr, 27, 117, 118
Beinn a' Bheithir, 30, 74
Beinn a'Bhuird, 26, 81, 101, 102, 137
Beinn Buidhe, 43
Beinn na Caillich, 67, 68, 74, 76
Beinn a' Chlaidheimh, 58, 59
Beinn Eighe, 19, 118
Beinn Eunaich, 108
Beinn a' Ghlo, 25
Beinn Lair, 74, 117, 118
Beinn Laoigh, 24
Beinn an Lochain, 64
Beinn Nuis, 120, 121, 145
Beinn an Oir, 28, 55, 67, 68, 74
Beinn Oss, 25
Beinn Tarsuinn, 57, 58
Beinn Trilleachan, 23, 167
Bell, Dr J.H.B., 137
Beltane Fires, 33
Ben Alder, 13, 48, 74, 132
Ben Avon, 13, 24, 67, 99, 100, 154
Ben Chonzie, 74, 153
Ben Cruachan, 31, 42, 74, 76, 157
Ben Hope, 118
Ben Klibreck, 66
Ben Lawers, 55, 59, 74-6, 150, 160, 181
Ben Ledi, 31, 33, 59, 74, 76
Ben Lomond, 25, 32, 33, 52, 60, 65-9, 74, 79, 109
Ben Loyal, 59, 102
Ben Macdhui, 53, 81, 101, 106, 111, 166
Ben More (Crianlarich), 51, 109
Ben More (Mull), 55, 69, 70, 74